Mastering Risk, Growth, and Value Creation
in Entrepreneurship

HER

Bold

BUSINESS MOVES

HANNA OLIVAS

ALONG WITH 14 INSPIRING AUTHORS

ISBN: 978-1-966798-61-3

TABLE OF CONTENTS

INTRODUCTION 5

Her Bold Business Moves: The Power of Being Bold in Business
  By Hanna Olivas 7

The Courage to Grow
  By Sharee Pack 14

The Bold Leap: Recognizing the Call to Something More
  By Heather Nielsen... 24

Being Original
  By Hunyah Irfan... 36

Blueprint of a Bold Woman
  By Lovely LaGuerre.. 43

Navigating Bold Business Moves Through Ancient Wisdom
  By Charel Morris 49

The Business Vision Is Yours
  By Dr. Nefertiti S Fisher 59

The Power of Collaboration & Affiliate Marketing in Business
  By Kayshaun Brooks.. 67

Embracing the Mindset of an Authorpreneur
  By Kimberly Tyler 75

Building Bridges: The Power of Networking in Bold Business Moves
  By Maureen Byers 84

The Dream Engineer Who Carved Her Own Path - A Light Worker's
Guide to Dancing with Agency
  By Gracy Goldman 90

The Quantum Dreams of Harmonix LLC
By Lillian Jaques 103

From Business to Stage: Embracing the Unexpected Path of
Reinvention
By Dr. Gina Kuhn-Robatin 109

Unapologetically Visible: The Bold Business Move That Changed
Everything
By Nana Adjoa Sifa Amponsah 115

Born to Reign
By Krizel Rodriguez 126

INTRODUCTION

In the world of entrepreneurship, taking risks isn't just a part of the journey—it's the essence of the journey itself. But what separates the ordinary from the extraordinary? It's the ability to embrace risk with purpose, navigate growth with agility, and unlock value that goes beyond financial metrics. This is what *Her Bold Business Moves* is all about: empowering women to master the core principles of risk, growth, and value creation in their entrepreneurial ventures.

This book isn't a traditional "how-to" guide. It's a dynamic roadmap that takes you through the complexities of modern business through the eyes of women who have not only survived but thrived in the ever-evolving entrepreneurial landscape. It tells the stories of women who've had the courage to make bold moves—whether that's investing in a game-changing idea, scaling their businesses in uncharted waters, or reinventing industries with innovative solutions.

The pages ahead offer insights into the strategic decisions, mindset shifts, and unique challenges faced by female entrepreneurs, while also providing actionable strategies and inspiring lessons to propel your own business ventures forward. From understanding the foundational aspects of risk management to leveraging growth opportunities and ultimately creating lasting value, *Her Bold Business Moves* arms you with the tools and confidence to tackle challenges head-on and lead with purpose.

As you turn these pages, you'll gain more than just business knowledge—you'll uncover the power within yourself to take bold, calculated steps towards building a business that doesn't just succeed, but truly makes an impact. This is your invitation to think bigger, move bolder, and make the kinds of decisions that will shape the future of your entrepreneurial journey.

The business world is waiting for your boldest moves. Are you ready to take them?

Hanna Olivas

Founder and CEO of SHE RISES STUDIOS

https://www.linkedin.com/company/she-rises-studios/
https://www.facebook.com/sherisesstudios
https://www.instagram.com/sherisesstudios_llc/
www.SheRisesStudios.com

Author, Speaker, and Founder. Hanna was born and raised in Las Vegas, Nevada, and has paved her way to becoming one of the most influential women of 2022. Hanna is the co-founder of She Rises Studios and the founder of the Brave & Beautiful Blood Cancer Foundation. Her journey started in 2017 when she was first diagnosed with Multiple Myeloma, an incurable blood cancer. Now more than ever, her focus is to empower other women to become leaders because The Future is Female. She is currently traveling and speaking publicly to women to educate them on entrepreneurship, leadership, and owning the female power within.

Her Bold Business Moves: The Power of Being Bold in Business

By Hanna Olivas

Bold. It's a word that carries so much weight, especially for women in business. To be bold means to take risks, to stand out, to do things differently—even when you don't know how it's going to turn out. It means owning your decisions, trusting your instincts, and embracing the unknown. But most importantly, it means stepping into your power, unapologetically, and knowing that you belong in the room.

When I look back at my journey as a business owner, the word bold resonates deeply with me. I've made some of the boldest moves in business, even when I wasn't sure how they would pan out. And while not every move was easy, each one taught me something invaluable: "It's okay to be bold in business. In fact, it's necessary if you want to succeed." Boldness isn't just about taking risks; it's about trusting yourself enough to take those risks and knowing that you can navigate whatever comes your way.

The Mental Strength of Being Bold

Being bold in business starts with your mindset. "Boldness begins in the mind—it's about believing in yourself and your ability to make things happen." There were many times in my journey when I doubted myself. When I thought, *What if this doesn't work? What if I fail?* But here's the thing: "Boldness isn't about eliminating fear—it's about moving forward in spite of it."

I remember the first time I made a bold business decision that scared me to my core. I was starting a new venture, and I knew it was risky. I had no guarantees that it would work, but I also knew that if I didn't take the leap, I would always wonder, *What if?* So, I chose boldness. I chose to trust myself, to believe in my vision, and to take the risk. And while there were challenges along the way, that decision ended up being one of the best moves I've ever made.

"Bold moves require bold thinking." That means you have to train your mind to think differently. You can't play small if you want to make big moves. You have to be willing to dream big, to think outside the box, and to take action on those dreams, even when they seem impossible. It's about having the courage to say, "I'm going to do this," and then backing that up with action.

One of the mantras I live by is "Doubt will creep in, but boldness drowns it out." Every time I feel that doubt creeping in, I remind myself that I've made bold moves before, and I can do it again. Boldness is a muscle, and the more you exercise it, the stronger it gets.

Emotional Resilience: The Heart of Boldness

Being bold in business isn't just about having a strong mindset—it's also about having emotional resilience. When you make bold moves, you're going to face setbacks. You're going to encounter moments when things don't go as planned, when you feel like you've hit a wall. And in those moments, it's easy to second-guess yourself. But here's what I've learned: "Boldness and resilience go hand in hand."

There have been times when I've made bold business moves that didn't turn out the way I hoped. I've had deals fall through, investments that didn't pay off, and projects that didn't hit the mark. And in those moments, it's easy to feel like giving up. But boldness isn't about never failing—it's about how you rise after you fall. "Every bold move, whether it succeeds or not, is an opportunity to learn, grow, and come back stronger."

I remember a time when I put everything on the line for a business deal that ended up falling apart at the last minute. I was devastated. I questioned whether I had made the right decision, whether I was cut out for this. But after some reflection, I realized something important: "Bold moves don't always lead to success, but they always lead to growth." That failed deal taught me resilience. It taught me how to navigate disappointment, how to pivot when things don't go as planned, and how to keep moving forward.

"Emotional resilience is the foundation of boldness—it's what allows you to keep going, even when the road gets tough." As women in business, we need to cultivate that resilience, to remind ourselves that we are capable of handling whatever comes our way. Boldness isn't about being fearless; it's about being brave enough to face your fears and keep going.

Physical Energy: Fueling Bold Moves

When we talk about being bold in business, we often focus on the mental and emotional aspects, but there's another critical component: physical energy. "Bold moves require energy—physical, mental, and emotional." To make bold decisions and follow through on them, you need to take care of your body just as much as you take care of your mind.

For me, maintaining my physical energy has been a game-changer in my business. Running a business, making big decisions, and navigating challenges all require stamina. "You can't be bold if you're running on empty." That's why I've made self-care a priority in my life. Whether it's exercise, eating well, or simply taking time to rest, I know that my physical health directly impacts my ability to show up as the bold, badass businesswoman I am.

There was a time in my life when I thought I could just push through, that I didn't need to slow down. But after hitting burnout more than once, I realized: "Being bold in business also means being bold enough to take care of yourself." It's not a weakness to rest—it's a strength. When you take care of your body, you're giving yourself the energy you need to make bold moves with clarity and confidence.

Asking for Help: A Bold Move in Itself

One of the boldest business moves I've ever made was asking for help. As women, we often feel like we have to do it all on our own, that asking for help is a sign of weakness. But let me tell you this: "Asking for help is one of the boldest, most empowering things you can do in business."

Early on in my entrepreneurial journey, I tried to do everything myself. I thought that being a successful business owner meant wearing all the hats and never asking for assistance. But as my business grew, I realized that trying to do it all was holding me back. I needed support, I needed guidance, and I needed to surround myself with people who could help me grow. "Boldness is knowing when to ask for help and being confident enough to accept it."

Asking for help allowed me to scale my business in ways I never could have imagined. It gave me the freedom to focus on what I do best and let others step in where I needed support. It also opened the door to mentorship and collaboration, which have been key in my growth as a business owner. "When you ask for help, you're not showing weakness—you're showing strength."

Boldness Is Bringing Others Along

One of the most important lessons I've learned on this journey is: "Boldness isn't just about rising on your own—it's about bringing others along with you." As women in business, we have a unique opportunity to lift each other up, to create spaces where other women can thrive, and to build communities of support.

I've always believed that my success is not just about me—it's about the women who are coming up behind me, the ones who are looking for someone to show them that it's possible. "When you make bold moves, you inspire others to do the same." That's why I've made it a priority to mentor other women, to share my knowledge, my experiences, and my mistakes, so they can learn and grow from them.

Boldness is contagious. When you see someone else making bold moves, it gives you the courage to do the same. I've seen it time and time again—when one woman steps into her power, it creates a ripple effect. "When you rise, bring others with you. That's the true mark of a bold leader."

Embracing Boldness in Every Decision

Being bold in business isn't just about making big, flashy moves—it's about embracing boldness in every decision you make, no matter how small. "Boldness is a mindset—it's about showing up with confidence, making decisions with intention, and trusting yourself to handle whatever comes next." Whether it's launching a new product, negotiating a deal, or simply setting boundaries in your business, every decision you make is an opportunity to be bold.

One of the boldest moves I've made in my business was pivoting when things weren't working. It wasn't easy to admit that I needed to change direction, but "boldness means being willing to course-correct when necessary." It means not being afraid to make tough decisions, even when they feel uncomfortable. That's how you grow. That's how you build a business that is not only successful but sustainable.

The Bold Woman You're Becoming

To every woman reading this, I want you to know that you have the power to be bold in business. You have the power to make bold moves, to take risks, and to trust yourself, even when the path ahead is uncertain. "Boldness is not about knowing the outcome—it's about having the courage to step forward anyway."

You don't have to have it all figured out. You don't have to wait for the perfect moment. Boldness is about taking action now, trusting that you'll figure it out as you go. "Bold moves create momentum, and momentum leads to growth." You don't have to be fearless to be bold.

You just have to be willing to step into the unknown, to believe in your vision, and to keep pushing forward, no matter what.

So, to the woman who's ready to embrace boldness, I want to leave you with this: "Be bold in everything you do, in every decision you make, and in every step you take toward your dreams. Your boldness is your power, and the world is waiting for you to rise."

Remember, being bold doesn't mean you won't face challenges. It doesn't mean you won't experience setbacks. But it does mean that you will continue to rise, that you will continue to make moves, and that you will create the life and business you deserve. You are a bold, badass woman in business, and your journey is just beginning.

"Boldness isn't about what you've done—it's about who you're becoming." And I can't wait to see the bold woman you're becoming.

Sharee Pack

Sharee Health
Radiant Energy Healer & Holistic Business Mentor

https://www.linkedin.com/in/shareerpack/
https://www.facebook.com/shareerpack
https://www.instagram.com/shareerpack
https://shareehealth.com/
https://automationblueprint.me/

Sharee Pack is a Radiant Energy Healer and Holistic Business Mentor, blending 40+ years of energy healing with cutting-edge business strategies. She specializes in clearing emotional and energetic blocks through Radiant Energy Healing, Reiki, Chinese meridians, EFT tapping, and chakra balancing, empowering clients to step into alignment and success. Beyond healing, Sharee helps entrepreneurs simplify tech systems, streamlining workflow so they can focus on what matters—growing passion and impact. Her journey into holistic wellness began at 14 when alternative medicine transformed her health. This sparked a lifelong mission to help others heal deeply, live radiantly, and build thriving businesses. A devoted wife, mother, and grandmother, Sharee cherishes faith, family, and holistic living. She loves strategy board games, laughter, and strengthening connections through play. Whether through energy work or tech solutions, Sharee helps clients release overwhelm and step into clarity, balance, and abundance—so they can thrive in life and business.

The Courage to Grow

By Sharee Pack

Trusting Your Gifts, Scaling with Ease, and Thriving

The Moment That Changed Everything

I lay in bed, staring at the ceiling, my body weak, my mind exhausted. How long had I been searching for answers? Over a year now, doctor after doctor had examined me, their expressions laced with sympathy but void of solutions. "We don't know what's wrong," they would say, and each time, their words deepened my fear. What if I never got better? What if I remained trapped in this fragile, unrecognizable version of myself?

More than the physical weakness, it was the helplessness that haunted me—the gnawing uncertainty of not knowing what lay ahead. The fear of never fully healing, of never reclaiming my life, was suffocating. I had always believed that if I just pushed through, if I just held on a little longer, the answers would come. But what if they didn't? What if I was stuck here, forever at the mercy of the unknown?

Then, something unexpected happened. My father, refusing to accept defeat, found a medical homeopathic doctor who introduced me to Chinese meridian healing. It was unconventional, something many would dismiss—but I was desperate. I remember skepticism mixing with hope working with this new practitioner. I didn't understand it, but for the first time in months, I felt something shift inside me—like a current of energy awakening. Over time, my strength returned, and with it, a realization: Healing wasn't just about medicine. It was about **trusting new possibilities.** That leap of faith into holistic healing didn't just restore my health; it planted the first seed of a much greater journey—my calling to help others heal.

From that moment on, I had a thirst to learn everything I could about holistic healing, energy work, meditation, EFT tapping, and Chinese meridians. My fascination grew deeper, and in my early 20s, I began working alongside holistic doctors, assisting them with their patients. It was a transformative experience—watching people regain their health, their energy, their zest for life. I witnessed firsthand the incredible potential of these healing modalities to bring vibrant health and a full life to others. As my passion grew, I pursued extensive training and became certified in multiple healing modalities. Each certification deepened my understanding, but more importantly, it reaffirmed that my calling was not just to learn but to help others experience true healing. The more I learned, the more I knew that this was the path I was meant to walk.

Yet years later, when I stepped into the world of holistic entrepreneurship, **that same fear returned.** The fear of the unknown, the fear of stepping into something unconventional, the fear of trusting myself. It was no longer about my body healing—it was about my **worthiness** in stepping forward as a healer. Who was I to do this? Would anyone take me seriously? The same doubts that once kept me trapped in uncertainty resurfaced. But just as I had trusted the unknown in my healing, I had to trust my gifts in my business.

The biggest breakthroughs always come from stepping into the unknown.

The Fear of Owning Your Expertise

When I first started my business, I hesitated to call myself an expert. Even though I had over 40 years of experience in energy healing— learning, practicing, and witnessing profound transformations—I still questioned myself. I kept thinking that maybe I needed one more certification, one more client success story, or one more external validation before I could truly claim my expertise. But when it came time to step forward as a professional, doubt gripped me. I would sit with my pricing sheet, my stomach twisting in knots, as a voice in my mind whispered, *Who do you think you are?*

I worried constantly. What if people thought I was charging too much? What if they questioned my credibility? What if they discovered that, despite all my training, I still had moments of uncertainty? I kept lowering my prices, believing that making it "affordable" would make me more worthy. But deep down, I knew the real issue wasn't money—it was my self-worth.

I see this all the time with heart-centered entrepreneurs. We are deeply connected to service, but we hesitate when it comes to charging for our work. We spend years earning certifications, mastering our craft, and proving ourselves, but still, there's a lingering doubt: *Am I really good enough?* It's as if we're waiting for someone else to validate our worth before we can own it ourselves.

I remember questioning whether I had "earned" the right to charge for my work. Even after years of training, I felt like I needed one more certification, one more client testimonial, one more sign that I was legitimate. But the truth is, **worthiness doesn't come from external validation—it comes from within.** I realized that no certificate or title could give me what I had to claim for myself: the belief that my work was powerful and deeply needed.

One day, a mentor said something that shifted everything for me: "People don't pay for your time; they pay for their transformation." That realization struck me to my core. I wasn't just offering sessions—I was offering healing, breakthroughs, and the opportunity for someone to step into a new reality. And when I finally stepped into that understanding, everything changed. My confidence grew, my pricing aligned with the impact I created, and most importantly, I saw how my shift empowered my clients to invest in their own transformation.

When we own our worth, we don't just lift ourselves—we create space for others to do the same. That's the ripple effect of recognizing our power. And I want you to feel that shift, too.

Reflection Prompt: *Have you ever hesitated to charge your worth or own your expertise? Why?*

Scaling Smart: Why Working Harder Isn't the Answer

In the early days of my business, I was doing everything manually— scheduling, invoicing, client follow-ups, marketing. I convinced myself that if I just worked harder, success would come. So, I worked. And worked. Night after night, I found myself staring at my computer screen well past midnight, my body aching, my mind exhausted. One a.m. turned into two, then three. I would catch a couple of hours of sleep, only to wake up and do it all over again. I was running on empty, pouring every ounce of energy into my business, believing that if I just pushed a little harder, I would finally break through.

But instead of freedom, I felt suffocated. Instead of growth, I felt stuck. The business I had built to create a better life had become a prison of my own making. I was trapped in a cycle of exhaustion with no way out. One night, in sheer frustration, I slammed my laptop shut and whispered into the darkness, "I was trying to create freedom, but all I've done is cage myself in."

It was in that moment that I realized something had to change. I wasn't meant to be drowning in work—I was meant to be thriving. That was the beginning of my shift from working harder to working smarter.

Tech was something I was naturally good at. I had always loved it. In fact, back in the 80s, I even took college courses in computer programming—C++, to be exact—thinking I might build a career in it. But as much as I loved coding, I realized that my heart was with people. I thrived on connection, on meaningful conversations, on guiding others through transformation. So, I stepped away from tech as a career, but it never fully left me.

One of my biggest struggles in business, though, was how I approached tech. Instead of investing in a solid system, I was piecing things together, chasing every free option I could find. I told myself I was being resourceful, but in reality, I was making things harder for myself. Juggling multiple platforms, trying to make disconnected tools talk to each other—it left me frustrated and drowning in unnecessary work.

The truth was, I wasn't willing to invest in my business, and deep down, that reflected something bigger: I wasn't fully seeing myself as worthy of success. It wasn't until I stepped away from the free and the patchwork solutions and invested in an all-in-one platform—one that allowed everything to flow seamlessly—that I finally experienced a sense of freedom in my business. This change revolutionized how I operated, allowing me to automate key processes while staying even more personal and connected with my clients.

That shift was about more than just tech. It was about stepping into a new level of self-worth—recognizing that I deserved to have a business that worked for me, not the other way around. And that realization led me to something even greater. After two years of using an all-in-one platform, I joined forces with three other incredible women, and together, we built Automation Blueprint—a customer relations platform that is all-in-one, designed to help female entrepreneurs automate their businesses, reclaim their time, and take their lives back.

Many entrepreneurs believe they must work harder to grow. The reality? Working smarter is the key to sustainable success.

I used to believe that if I just worked a little harder, if I just put in a few more late nights, then everything would finally fall into place. But the harder I worked, the deeper I sank into exhaustion, constantly chasing an invisible finish line that kept moving further away. The moment I realized that more effort wasn't the answer—that working smarter was—I felt both relief and resistance. Could I really build success without burning myself out? Could I trust that I was still earning my success by automating, delegating, and setting boundaries?

It wasn't easy to shift my mindset, but when I did, everything changed. I learned that success doesn't come from sacrificing yourself—it comes from building systems that allow you to grow without breaking down. Once I embraced this, my business and my life transformed. I finally stepped into the freedom I had been working so hard to create all along.

Action Step: *Identify one task in your business that could be automated or streamlined. What small step can you take today?*

The Growth Mindset: Turning Challenges Into Stepping Stones

Every entrepreneur faces obstacles—failed launches, slow months, tech hiccups. The key isn't avoiding challenges; it's learning how to navigate them. I remember when I poured my heart into my first masterclass, convinced that it would be a game-changer. I had spent weeks crafting the content, refining the messaging, and preparing to deliver immense value. The night before the launch, I could hardly sleep. I was filled with excitement, anticipation, and a hint of nervous energy.

But when the launch day came, I opened my email... and saw nothing. No sign-ups. Not a single one. My heart sank. A wave of self-doubt crashed over me: *Maybe I wasn't meant to do this. Maybe I had misunderstood my calling. What if people just didn't see value in what I had to offer?*

I wanted to shut down my laptop and walk away. The disappointment felt crushing, like a confirmation of every lingering fear I had about stepping into this work. But then, through the frustration and doubt, another thought emerged: *What is this challenge teaching me?* Instead of seeing it as a failure, I treated it as feedback. I took a deep breath, reassessed my approach, tweaked my messaging, refined my offer, and tried again.

The next time, the response was completely different. People showed up. They engaged. They invested. And I realized something profound— **every challenge is preparing us for the next level.** That first "failure" wasn't a sign to quit. It was a lesson in resilience, refinement, and the power of trying again.

Jim Rohn once said, "For things to change, you have to change." That quote hit me hard. I had been so focused on external success that I hadn't looked inward. I had to change how I viewed failure, how I viewed growth, and most importantly, how I viewed myself. The moment I embraced that, I stopped waiting for things to get easier—I became stronger. That shift not only transformed my business but gave me the courage to continue stepping forward, no matter the obstacles.

Reflection Prompt: *What's one challenge in your business that you can reframe as a growth opportunity?*

The Bold Move Challenge: Taking Inspired Action

There comes a moment in every entrepreneur's journey when they stand at a crossroads. One path feels familiar—staying in the comfort of what they know, waiting for the perfect time, hoping clarity will arrive before they act. The other path? It's filled with uncertainty, but it's also where the biggest breakthroughs happen.

I know this moment well. I've felt the hesitation, the inner debate between staying safe and stepping boldly into the unknown. There were times I told myself I wasn't ready—that I needed more training, more proof, more validation before I could take my next step. But what I've learned is this: Clarity doesn't come before action. It comes because of action.

The boldest moves in my business—the ones that truly changed everything—weren't made when I felt fully prepared. They were made when I decided to trust myself, even in the face of uncertainty. When I raised my prices for the first time, invested in automation to scale smarter, and stopped over-explaining my value and simply owned it, those moments propelled me forward.

Your Bold Move Challenge

Right now, I want you to ask yourself: *What is one bold business move I've been avoiding?*

Is it raising your prices? Launching that offer you've been sitting on? Hiring support? Automating a system that's draining your time? Whatever it is, take that step this week. Not next month. Not next quarter. This week.

Will it feel uncomfortable? Probably. **But that discomfort is not a stop sign—it's a sign of growth.**

Your Time Is Now

The boldest moves lead to the biggest growth. You are capable, ready, and closer than you think. Don't let fear or hesitation keep you from stepping into the next level of your success. Take the step. Make the move.

Because everything you want is on the other side of action.

Next Steps: How to Continue Your Growth

One of the ways I was able to keep growing was through meditation and journaling. These practices became my anchor, allowing me to reflect, reset, and align with my vision. I want to help you on your journey as well. That's why I've created a special gift for you—a meditation and journaling guide designed to support your growth and help you step fully into your power. You can access it here: [Insert Link].

For those who want to continue this journey, I invite you to connect with me at shareehealth.com. Surround yourself with those who lift you higher. Keep growing, keep thriving, and most importantly—keep believing in your gifts.

✨ *"Your next level is waiting. The only question is—are you ready to take the leap?"*

Heather Nielsen

My Divine Joy
Speaker, Mentor & Business Coach

https://www.linkedin.com/in/heathernielsen/
https://www.facebook.com/Heather2494/
https://www.instagram.com/nielsen.heather/
https://mydivinejoy.com/
https://www.choosingwisdom.org/

Heather Nielsen is a speaker, mentor, and business coach dedicated to helping women build thriving businesses while embracing the gift of motherhood. As a mother of five, she understands the challenges of balancing ambition with family life. Heather believes that true success—both in life and business—begins with inner work. We naturally achieve greater success, fulfillment, and impact when we heal, grow, and align with our purpose. Heather mentors faith-driven women in business strategy and personal development, equipping them with the mindset, confidence, and practical skills to create prosperous, purpose-filled businesses without sacrificing what matters most. She empowers women to break through limiting beliefs and achieve their highest potential with clarity, confidence, and joy—guiding them through her coaching, workshops, and speaking engagements. She lives in northern Utah with her husband, family, and pet bearded dragon. Discover how you can rise in both business and life at MyDivineJoy.com.

The Bold Leap: Recognizing the Call to Something More

By Heather Nielsen

"So, I guess what I'm asking is for you to take over the Choosing Wisdom blog."

Lori's words hung in the air, and for a moment, I wasn't sure I had heard her right.

Just weeks earlier, my world had been turned upside down. We were still grieving my ex-husband's suicide, navigating the impossible weight of loss, and trying to find our footing again. My two oldest boys from my first marriage needed me more than ever. Their father was gone, and I had to be strong for them while still managing the responsibilities of daily life.

On top of that, I had a baby in diapers—my youngest of three more children from my second marriage. Our home was filled with both grief and the beautiful chaos of motherhood, and I was doing everything I could to hold it all together.

And now, here was an opportunity I had never expected—an invitation to step into something that felt both terrifying and aligned.

A blog? A website? My own coaching business was just getting started— I was supposed to be building that, not taking on someone else's!

Every logical part of me said this was crazy. I should say no. It wasn't the right time. I wasn't prepared.

But deep inside, something nudged me forward.

I took a few deep breaths, closed my eyes, and whispered a simple prayer: *What am I supposed to do?*

And then, an idea.

"Maybe I could do this... with my best friend."

I grabbed my phone and called her. She was so excited, and we became co-founders of a business I had no idea how to run.

Just like that, I had taken a bold leap into the unknown.

The First Risk: Taking the Leap Before Feeling Ready

I had made the decision. I was officially stepping into this completely unknown territory of running Choosing Wisdom.

And almost immediately, the weight of everything I didn't know came crashing down.

Tech has never been my strength. Websites? Email campaigns? Social media strategies? I was a former high school physics teacher, not a digital marketing expert. I had spent years in coaching and personal development, but suddenly, I found myself staring at a screen filled with confusing backend settings, wondering what I had just agreed to.

There were moments—many moments—where doubt crept in.

"What if I fail? What if I ruin everything Lori built? What if I'm not smart enough to figure this out?"

I knew these thoughts weren't serving me. I had spent years coaching women on mindset and success, and yet, here I was, battling the same inner resistance that I had helped others overcome.

That's when I knew I needed to use my own tools.

I sat down and wrote out a simple affirmation that I repeated to myself every single day:

"Every day, I am learning and getting better. Learning new things comes easily to me."

At first, it felt ridiculous. I didn't believe it. But I had studied how the mind works, and I knew that the more I repeated something, the more my brain would start to accept it as truth.

So, I said it. Over and over.

Every time I struggled to understand a new tech tool—*"Every day, I am learning and getting better."*

Every time an email sequence didn't send properly—*"Learning new things comes easily to me."*

Every time I wanted to quit—*"I can figure this out."*

And slowly, something shifted.

I started figuring things out. The tech didn't seem as overwhelming. I learned how to schedule emails, create social media content, and keep the blog running.

Was it perfect? Absolutely not.

But I was taking action, learning as I went, and proving to myself that I was capable.

Looking back, I see now that this wasn't just about running a blog. This was the first of many bold business moves I would make—the first of many times I would say "yes" before I felt fully ready and trust that I would figure it out along the way.

☞ **Practical Exercise:** *What is something you've been avoiding because you don't feel ready? Write an affirmation that helps shift your mindset and commit to repeating it daily for the next week.*

Overcoming the Fear & Perfectionism That Holds Us Back

The irony of the timing wasn't lost on me.

Not only was I taking over Choosing Wisdom, learning tech I had never touched before, and figuring out how to manage a blog and email list, but I was also in the middle of my first coaching business training—the kind that forced me to answer big questions like:

"Who is my ideal client?"
"What exactly am I offering?"
"How do I even run a business?"

It was a lot. Too much, at times.

I felt like I was moving painfully slow, as if every step forward took twice the effort it should.

Then, one day, while listening to a training by Denise Duffield-Thomas, something clicked. She told a story about how she wrote her first book by announcing the release date before the book was even finished.

Her reasoning?

Once the date was out there, she had to follow through.

That hit me right in the gut.

Here I was, hesitating. Overthinking. Worrying that I wasn't ready.

But what if I just set a date and figured it out along the way?

So, I took a bold lesson from Denise and did something that felt completely terrifying:

I announced that I was teaching my first mini-course, Happier for the Holidays, and that it was happening in November.

Did I have everything built yet? Nope.

Did I know exactly how it would go? Not really.

But did I trust that I would show up and make it valuable? Absolutely.

And you know what?

People registered.
I showed up.
I taught the course.
And it was fantastic.

Not only did it serve people in the moment, but it's something I still share today inside my *Wealth & Wisdom Library*. It's not just about the holidays—it's about aligning with your values, overcoming negative thoughts, and improving relationships year-round.

Looking back, I realize that this was one of the biggest lessons of my entrepreneurial journey:

Taking imperfect action beats waiting for perfection. Every. Single. Time.

Had I waited until I "felt ready," Happier for the Holidays never would have happened.

Had I waited until I "knew everything" about running a blog Choosing Wisdom would have fizzled.

Momentum creates clarity.

That moment taught me that bold business moves aren't about having everything figured out first. They're about deciding, taking action, and trusting yourself to deliver.

👉 **Practical Exercise:** *Think of something you've been delaying because you don't feel ready. Set a date. Announce it. Commit to following through—even if you don't have all the details figured out yet.*

When the Pivot Becomes Clear: Following Your Energy & Passion

It was 2023, and I had signed up for a new program—one designed to help entrepreneurs make $10K in 30 days. Like every training I had taken before, I was fully invested in learning, growing, and applying what I was being taught.

I didn't go into that business training expecting to change my entire business model. But looking back, I can see now that it was the moment everything shifted.

One of our assignments was to practice our client discovery calls with other women in the cohort.

I went through my mock first-time coaching session. It went well. I felt confident.

But what happened after? That's when everything changed.

Once the "official" training part was over, we started casually chit-chatting about our individual businesses.

And that's when it happened. A light-bulb moment so big, I could almost hear the *click*.

As we talked, I felt pure joy helping these women see how they could make more money, stop undercharging, and truly value their work. I could see where they were holding themselves back and what they weren't charging enough for. And without even thinking, I started coaching them through their pricing, mindset, and business models.

That's when I realized—I loved this.

I had spent years coaching women on positivity and success.
I had taken tons of training on running a business.
And now, I could combine everything I had learned to help women with their businesses.

It was enlightening.

It was exciting.

And, honestly? It was a little terrifying.

Because imposter syndrome showed up fast.

"Really? Can I do this?"
"I'm still taking business trainings—who am I to coach others?"
"What if I'm not as good as the mentors I've learned from?"

That's when I remembered something from years ago, back when I was getting my Intuitive Mentoring Certification.

One of my coaches shared a powerful analogy that stuck with me:

"We're all swimming in a big pond, but the water isn't crystal clear. Right now, you're learning from me—but there are fish below you that can't even see me. They can only see you. And those are the people you're meant to serve."

That image hit me hard.

Because the truth is—we don't have to be the biggest fish in the pond to help someone.

There are women right now who can't see my mentors, but they can see me. They resonate with my story, my journey, my voice.

And those are the women I am meant to serve.

That realization was the turning point.

That was the big pivot.

I wasn't just a positivity coach.

I wasn't just a success coach.

I was now a business coach, too.

☞ **Practical Exercise:** *Think about the people who are just a few steps behind you in your journey. What knowledge or experience do you have* *that could help them? Write down one way you can share your wisdom with them—whether through a conversation, a post, a training, or an offer.*

Growth Is Intentional: The Power of Investing in Yourself

I have always been a reader—someone who finds joy in learning from the most intelligent and brilliant minds by diving into their books. Books are such an incredible gift. For just a few dollars, you can learn from some of the most successful, accomplished people in the world.

For decades, I devoured their stories, insights, and strategies. Reading became a form of mentorship for me. But eventually, I realized that books alone weren't enough.

I needed more than inspiration and theory—I needed accountability, feedback, and someone who could tell me, "Here's where you're holding back."

There came a point in my journey where I knew I had to find mentors— real people who had already walked the path I wanted to walk. Women who had built businesses with purpose and heart. Coaches who had made the leap from dreaming to doing.

I realized that I could **accelerate** my success by learning directly from those who had been there, done that, and were willing to show me how.

It wasn't just about information anymore—it was about transformation. And that required relationships, guidance, and proximity to people who could challenge me, stretch me, and believe in me even when I doubted myself.

Back in 2008, I was a real estate agent who hadn't made much money. I knew I needed to learn the business side of the industry.

So, for the first time, I hired a real estate coach.

I was excited to learn the strategies that would make me a better entrepreneur. And I did learn.

That real estate coach was only the beginning.

Since then, I have invested tens of thousands of dollars in continuing education, trainings, workshops, webinars, courses, and personal coaching.

And honestly? <u>It's been worth every penny.</u>

Because what I've learned is this:

- **Growth isn't accidental.**
- **It doesn't just happen.**
- **It requires intentional choices.**

And the best part? Change happens faster than we think it will.

Looking back, I'm in awe of how much I've grown in a relatively short amount of time.

It's amazing what can happen when we:

- Make the decision to grow
- Take intentional action
- Surround ourselves with mentors and knowledge that challenge us to be better

And that's exactly what I want for every woman reading this.

☞ **Practical Exercise:** *Take a moment to reflect on the last time you invested in your own growth—whether it was a book, a course, a coach, or even just a decision to push yourself forward. Now, think about what your next step could be. Where do you want to grow next? Write it down—and commit to taking action.*

You Are More Ready Than You Think

If there's one thing I've learned from my own journey, it's this:

- **You don't need more time.**
- **You don't need more credentials.**
- **You don't need permission.**

You are already equipped with everything you need to take your next bold business move.

Looking back, every major breakthrough in my life happened before I felt "ready."

I wasn't "ready" to take over Choosing Wisdom—but I did it anyway.

I wasn't "ready" to run my first online course—yet I put it out there and figured it out.

I wasn't "ready" to pivot into business coaching—until I realized that my years of learning had already prepared me for it.

And here's what I know now:

Your next level will require you to take action before you feel 100% ready. Your impact will grow the moment you fully own your gifts and stop holding back.
The people you are meant to serve are already looking for you—they just need you to step up and shine.

The Power of the Pivot & the Call to Rise

One of the biggest lessons I've learned is that growth requires pivots.

You will outgrow old roles.
You will feel the nudge to shift.
You will face moments where the path ahead feels uncertain.

But uncertainty is not a reason to stop.

If I had ignored my calling to expand into business coaching, I would have stayed in a place that no longer fit.

And if I had let fear dictate my choices, I wouldn't be here today—helping women like you step into your own brilliance.

Your Next Bold Move Starts Now

So now, it's your turn.

- What is the bold move you've been putting off?
- What is the pivot you know you need to make?
- Where have you been waiting to feel "ready" when deep down, you already know it's time?

I challenge you to take one step today.

Not next week.
Not next year.
Not when the timing is "perfect."

Right now!

Because the truth is: Success isn't about being the most prepared. It's about being the most willing to take action.

The world needs your message.
Your people are waiting for you.
Your next level is already calling.

☞ **Final Practical Exercise:** *Write down one bold business move you've been avoiding. Commit to taking action on it within the next seven days. Even if it's small, even if it's messy—just move forward. Then, reflect on how that action shifts your energy and confidence.*

Hunyah Irfan

Hunyah Travels
Content Creator

https://ca.linkedin.com/in/hunyah-irfan-blogger351
https://www.facebook.com/OfficialHunyahTravels
https://www.instagram.com/officalhunyahtravels
https://www.youtube.com/@officalhunyahtravels1

Hunyah is a content creator with a community development background. Hunyah currently facilitates with the University of Toronto CACHE program. Hunyah has worked on different content creation projects from halal ribfest 2024 to various projects. Hunyah will be talking about her business got to where it is today.

Being Original

By Hunyah Irfan

Hi, my name is Hunyah, and I'm from Brampton, Ontario.

I would like to discuss with you today about being original in your business.

Being a content creator in a way, a freelancer, but also an independent contract instructor.

There have been challenges for me.

Yes, I'm successful with where I'm today, as HunyahTravels.

But my challenges were not easy.

Today, I'm sharing with you my experiences of being a content creator and how I got to be where I am today with my saying, "Be original."

These topics I will discuss with you today.

1. Navigating through Google
2. On your own
3. Keeping up with expenses

Navigating Through Google

As you know, being a businesswoman is hard.

Along my journey as a content creator, it was not easy.

There is a problem that I come across a lot through my work.

That is Google.

Yes, Google is good.

But the problem is if you search yourself.

The results you will find will confuse people.

Years ago, in my early 20s, I got misguided into using Amazon self-publishing to pursue my personal problem through writing.

That personal problem was a romantic relationship that took 10 years to end and didn't end well.

I don't want to discuss this romantic relationship.

At the end of that relationship was Google.

That is because my significant other and I were mistakenly everywhere on Google.

It was unintentional how Google came in.

But this bothered me a lot.

Yet the relationship did end, but not the problem with Google.

It's been about 6 years since the Google problem. But it's still there.

This was a problem for me because, when I first began doing food reviews, whoever would Google me would find my significant other and me, not HunyahTravels.

That was very challenging.

But the good news I found a way through.

That was actually my food reviews.

The food reviews actually let go of the previous Google results.

Even today, I get asked sometimes about my significant other of which ended because of Google.

But now it doesn't show up in that situation.

The good news, it shows up on HunyahTravels reviews.

That was a great challenge at the start of being a content creator.

It was not easy.

Any entrepreneur who knows, if you see Google, then you would know.

Whether it's to have your business there or not.

On Your Own

If you think I had supportive people starting as a content creator, honestly, I didn't know.

When I first started on small content creation projects, and also doing small food reviews before leading up to the Ribfest in 2024.

Surprisingly, a lot of people were not there for me.

I remember when I first won my competition in 2022.

I learned that many of my family and friends tried to ruin my chances of winning or something, even going for the next goal in my life at that time.

I remember being told by a lot of people that I don't have the potential to be in the career that I want.

This was bullying in a way.

But once I stopped talking to family and friends who brought me down at the time.

It was just my prayers that got me to where I am today.

To do in-person spoken word events, being a summit speaker, and now writing my chapter about being original.

Honestly, I did cry a lot at times when I didn't have the potential, but I don't have the face that people are looking for.

Too short.

No experience.

When really something did need you, just try not to have a face that people are looking for.

As a woman entrepreneur, I have a huge problem with having no one to support me in food reviews, content creation, or spoken word events.

Now, surprisingly, those people look up to me.

It was just faith in this.

Keeping Up with Expenses

Being an entrepreneur, expenses are not easy.

That is because you have to see how you invest and what you gain from this.

When I first started my merchandise for donations, I spent a lot on the material.

I wanted to do something more than social media ads.

I found Vistaprint can do my merchandise.

That merchandise was like pens and water bottles.

Like little things

But mistakenly, I spent a lot of my money at the time on Vistaprint.

In 2022, at that time, I didn't know.

In 2025, I got to know the merchandise websites where you can earn and create your own merchandise.

That was my worst mistake.

Now, I actually have a merchandise store.

In those days, I didn't know.

This financial mistake I learned from showed me where to spend my money and where to look for options.

These are my bold business moves. I hope you learned something.

I hope my journey will be inspirational for a new entrepreneur.

Thank you

Lovely LaGuerre

Pure Heavenly Hair and Beauty Boutique
Wealth Creator, Best Selling Author &
Strategies Coach To Thrive In Life and Business

https://www.linkedin.com/in/lovelylaguerre/
https://m.facebook.com/pureheavenlyhairboutique
https://www.instagram.com/pureheavenlyhair
https://www.lovelyinspireyou.com
http://www.pureheavenlyhair.com
https://lovelysellsvegas.com

Lovely LaGuerre is a Wealth Creator Amazon Best Seller and a Business Strategist.

Lovely leads life with purpose and believe in leveling the plane fields in business and in personal life. Keep thriving in your business and collaborate with like minded individuals.

Having An Unstoppable Woman Mindset Lovely shares her story that will inspire, motivate, and empower you.

Lovely is on a mission to help others to thrive in their business and building their legacy.

She's also the Founder/Owner of Pure Heavenly Hair & Beauty Boutique, a luxury beauty brand that will transforming, inspiring, and empowering women to unleash their beauty inside and out.

Lovely has a passion for supporting and empowering other women. She believes that together women can become unstoppable by leveraging their potential and giving back to their communities. She is a member of CALV, NAR, and LVR Association, and many more.

Additionally, Lovely is mission is looking to collaborate on podcast series dedicated to motivating and empowering women, through sharing their journey with other fellow female entrepreneurs. She is a member of CALV, NAR, and LVR Association, and many more.

Blueprint of a Bold Woman

By Lovely LaGuerre

Building Beyond Limits, Leading With Legacy

I never planned on becoming the blueprint I became one by necessity.

Not because I had it all figured out, but because I couldn't ignore the pull to create something bigger than comfort, deeper than success, and more meaningful than money. The truth is, I didn't start out bold. I became bold by deciding I wouldn't let fear write the story of my life.

Entrepreneurship wasn't just a career move it was a calling. And once I answered it, everything changed.

The Moment I Chose to Begin

There's always a moment. Mine came quietly, in the middle of an ordinary day when I realized I could no longer live in survival mode I yearned for something more, mentally, creatively, and financially. I knew I was capable of more, destined for more, *meant* for more.

Moreover, me wanting more is only the first step. Choosing it? That takes grit.

So, I did what bold women do I moved without having every answer. I chose possibility over predictability. I chose to build, even though I didn't yet know how.

And that one decision to stop waiting and start walking became the cornerstone of my empire.

Risk as My Refiner

The world romanticizes risk, but real risk? It's lonely. It's messy. It's humbling.

There were times I took leaps with trembling hands and a whisper of faith. I invested in things that didn't pay off right away. I made mistakes that cost me time, energy, and sleep. But I kept moving. Giving up was not an option.

Because every risk, even the painful ones, refined me. They made me sharper, wiser, stronger. I started seeing risk not as a threat, but as an invitation to grow, to trust the process, most importantly believing in myself, and to evolve as a woman and as a leader.

The truth? Every bold move I've made was less about certainty and more about alignment. I moved not because I knew it would work but because I *knew I was ready to become the woman who could make it work.*

Growth Isn't Always Loud

There's a quiet kind of growth no one talks about. It happens when you're not being celebrated. When the wins are internal. When you're healing old mindsets, learning new strategies, and still showing up day after day without applause.

I had to grow past outdated beliefs, past limitations that were never mine to carry, and past the fear that I wasn't good enough, experienced enough, or *ready*.

I outgrew environments that couldn't hold the weight of my vision. I let go of relationships that didn't support the woman I was becoming. I started building from the inside out, a forward mindset, structure systems, strategy, and never stop creating.

And that kind of growth? It doesn't just expand your business. It transforms your life.

Value as My Voice

From day one, I didn't want to just make sales I wanted to make *statements*. I wanted to deliver value that echoed. That shifted something in people. That helped them *believe* in themselves again and bring the best out of themselves.

My business became the vehicle, but my voice was the engine.

I built brands rooted in truth, aligned with service, and elevated by excellence. I listened. I refined. I added depth to the way I showed up. I didn't just create offers I created *experiences*. And those experiences became the bridge between trust and transformation.

I wasn't here to blend in. I was here to raise the standard. And when you lead with real value, you never have to beg for loyalty. You *become* the brand people trust.

The Pivot Is Sacred

There came a moment when everything I had built no longer matched where I was going.

That's the part of the journey many don't prepare you for the moment when your own growth outpaces your current structure. I had to pivot. Not because I failed, but because I had outgrown my original vision.

And that's sacred.

I reimagined what success looked like. I repositioned my brand, redefined my market, and recommitted to my mission. I automated what I could. Delegated what I should. And focused on what only *I* could do: lead.

The pivot wasn't a setback. It was a rebirth. One that brought alignment, clarity, and overflow.

Legacy Over Limitation

This journey has never been about proving myself. It's always been about building something that would live beyond me.

Legacy, to me, is built in the unseen moments the hard decisions, the quiet leadership, the daily discipline. It's in the way you treat people, the culture you create, and the courage you carry.

I'm not just building wealth I'm building *worth*. I'm not just chasing goals I'm creating generational impact.

And I don't take that lightly.

That's why I mentor women who remind me of my former self ambitious, capable, and unsure if she's really "ready." I teach her that readiness is a myth. That power comes in the doing. And that the world doesn't need another perfect woman. It needs a present one.

My Bold Woman Blueprint

Here's the blueprint I've lived by written in moments of triumph and trial, sealed with resilience and refined through fire:

- **Decide fast. Grow slow.** Don't wait for perfect. Start now. Refine as you rise.
- **Invest in what multiplies.** Time, energy, people, and systems that expand your impact.
- **Stay in integrity.** With your vision, your voice, your values.
- **Lead with your heart, build with your hands.** Vision without execution is just a dream.
- **Be your own rescue.** Don't wait to be saved. Lead yourself, boldly and beautifully. After all you are the captain of your ship.

To the Woman Reading This You Are the Blueprint

If you're standing on the edge of something new, unsure if you're qualified to build it hear me when I say:

You don't need more time. You need more *truth*.

You are already equipped. Already worthy. Already more than enough.

Your blueprint isn't outside of you. It's *within* you. Written in your resilience, shaped by your experiences, and powered by your purpose.

You are the bold move. Live boldly in your truth.

Charel Morris

Founder of Stone Circle Productions

https://www.linkedin.com/in/charel/
https://www.facebook.com/profile.php?id=61565048890800
https://www.instagram.com/cybershaman/
https://www.cosmicquantumshaman.com/home

Charel is a spiritual catalyst and business visionary who masterfully integrates shamanic wisdom with modern leadership practices. Drawing from ancestral knowledge and quantum healing methodologies, she guides professionals beyond conventional business strategies into realms of deeper purpose and profound transformation. Through Sacred Shamanic Business Integration, she creates powerful containers where leaders experience breakthrough results while honoring their authentic gifts. Her unique approach addresses core patterns while unlocking extraordinary potential, helping clients achieve both professional excellence and meaningful impact. With a rare blend of strength and gentleness, Charel particularly resonates with purpose-driven entrepreneurs and executives seeking aligned success. Beyond individual work, she facilitates the Circle of EarthKeepers, a community dedicated to healing collective consciousness and supporting Earth's thriving. Charel embodies the perfect integration of ancient wisdom and business acumen—standing firmly in her truth while helping others discover theirs.

Navigating Bold Business Moves Through Ancient Wisdom

By Charel Morris

Who Am I?

I am a powerful yet gentle force, walking through life with authenticity and grace. In a world of digital platforms and virtual connections, I stand firmly grounded in my truth while remaining open-hearted and real. My strength flows from my ability to be both warrior and nurturer, leader and friend.

And here is what I do...

The winds whipped across the Las Vegas hotel rooftop as our small circle gathered under the night sky. Twelve people, drums in hand, had followed me here with nothing but trust and a shared intention. The conference below us—one that had grown from 113 attendees to 785 over seven years—faced an invisible threat no spreadsheet could solve.

What began as a tight-knit community of security professionals was being infiltrated by local party-seekers with no interest in our purpose. They came for the cheap admission ($40 for three days) and stayed for the chaos they created. Core members were threatening to abandon the event, saying it no longer held the magic that had defined it for years.

The conference creator had limited options. Raising prices slightly wouldn't deter the troublemakers. Close friends were not planning to stay if they showed up! Either way, he is risking a financial disaster.

I called my boss; he knew my work in ancient healing. I had an idea. He had no questions, his voice was clear: "Do what you think will work."

As our ceremony reached its climax, the drums echoing across the rooftop, something remarkable happened—the fierce desert wind simply stopped. Complete stillness enveloped us. Mother Earth herself acknowledged our work was done.

The next morning, walking through the conference hall, I could feel the transformation. We had energetically grown up about 10 years, overnight. Attendees stopped me throughout the conference, remarking on the palpable shift in energy. "It feels like the early years again," one longtime participant said. Others whispered about "the Shaman on the roof," a story already becoming legend within our community.

That year, the disruptive element mysteriously disappeared. Though we lost about a thousand local attendees, we gained fifteen hundred aligned new participants. Within three years, this event that nearly collapsed grew to just under 15,000 dedicated members.

No conventional business strategy could have produced this outcome. No pricing model or policy change could have preserved the community's essence while enabling its growth. Yet ceremonies will change the person or the tribe. This is the power of Sacred Shamanic Business Integration—addressing the energetic foundation of business challenges when material solutions fall short.

Introduction: Where Business Meets Spirit

This integration creates a revolutionary yet fluid approach to entrepreneurship by recognizing something most business schools never teach: your business has a spirit. Just as you carry your own unique energetic signature, your business emanates its own consciousness, purpose, and resonance.

Some of you may find this concept startling—perhaps even bizarre— while others might feel a wave of recognition washing over you, a quiet voice whispering, "Yes, I've sensed this all along." When you open yourself to the possibility that your business exists as more than spreadsheets and strategies—when you learn to commune with its spirit and weave its energy into your decisions—your entire approach to entrepreneurship transforms.

This isn't metaphorical language or a poetic way of discussing business intuition. And we have known for a long time that everything... EVERYTHING is energy. Your business truly exists as an energetic entity, born from your vision but evolving into something with its own essence, if you open to it. Learning to dance with this spirit provides guidance that illuminates everything from daily choices to pivotal decisions and rapid pivots when the market shifts beneath your feet, yet most never step in and dance.

I have been dancing around this for over 50 years in different ways. All I ask of you is to open and let the stories and words flow in so you can open to the powerful and sacred ways you can lift your business up. In the pages that follow, we'll explore how Sacred Shamanic Business Integration approaches the three pillars of entrepreneurial success—risk-taking, strategic growth, and value creation—through a perspective that honors both ancient wisdom and modern business demands.

I am not asking you to throw down your business practices or the wonderful education you have. I see a blend, not a takeover.

I started by telling you who I am—words and thoughts from my heart, my soul, and desire, so I would love for you to open up as you read and discover or create a short statement of Who You Are. You will find some points of reflections as we approach the three pillars as we move through this chapter.

Reflection #1: *When was the last time you felt a deep knowing about your business that transcended logical analysis? How did your body register this knowing—a warmth in your chest, a tingling at the base of your spine, a sudden clarity of vision? What are the two words that capture that moment? Your authentic presence will awaken the connection between your presence and the spirit of your project. And with that, you step fully into being an entrepreneurial woman.*

Risk-Taking: Trusting the Unknown Through Multidimensional Wisdom

When facing decisions where the path forward disappears into fog, conventional business approaches often leave us stranded. Spreadsheets and market analyses illuminate only what has been seen. Eventually, we all reach the threshold of the unknown—a space many entrepreneurs experience as a tightening in the chest, a heaviness that comes with the burden of decision.

Yet through the lens of Shamanic Journeying, the unknown isn't to be feared but rather an infinite possibilities and one is known as the Multiverse.

Accessing Your Multiverse Self

Every business encounters moments when solutions seem impossible to grasp—challenges that consume not just resources but the vital energy that fuels your vision. In these immovable moments, my client heads for Multiverse.

A basic description of the Multiverse is that there are an infinite number of Earths, and a version of you is on each one.

When you want guidance or support, you journey out and shift time and move to see the Multiverse and look or sense or vision the time universe out there and move to it. From there, you meet yourself and ask for guidance, healing, or help, depending on what you need. Sounds simple, but it will take time at first.

The Multiverse isn't merely a theoretical concept discussed by quantum physicists but an accessible field of possibilities waiting for your conscious engagement.

I guide my client to discover the path, moving away from "living on" Earth time. The sense or vision of the Multiverse becomes clear. And now she senses or hears or sees which universe is just waiting for her arrival. And with that, the fun begins.

Your Quantum Self as Guide

For other challenges, connecting with what I call your Quantum Self offers a different kind of clarity. This aspect of your consciousness exists beyond individual lifetimes—the thread of awareness that knows the full tapestry of your soul's journey.

Your Quantum Self perceives the trajectory of your highest purpose and can illuminate immediate practical matters with uncanny precision. I've witnessed entrepreneurs access this guidance to locate critical missing documents before high-stakes meetings, identify hidden flaws in seemingly promising partnership agreements, and discover marketing approaches that resonate at a frequency perfectly aligned with their deeper purpose.

Also, magic for finding car keys!

While the Multiverse approach connects you with parallel versions of your current self-navigating similar challenges, your Quantum Self provides guidance from a perspective outside the entire system, like the difference between asking a fellow hiker about the trail ahead versus consulting someone who has flown over the entire mountain range and sees all possible paths.

Reflection #2: *As you move through the world, how do you want your essence to be experienced by others? What qualities do you embody when you're standing fully in your power? Gather these words, let them resonate in your body until they feel absolutely right.*

Strategic Growth: When Walking Backward Moves You Forward

While conventional business wisdom fixates on continual forward momentum—bigger, faster, more— the spirit of your business recognizes that sometimes, the most powerful growth spirals rather than marches in a straight line. This may require embracing the teaching from a sacred contrarian who sees and acts from a perspective that appears backward but essentially contains profound wisdom.

My rooftop ceremony story illustrates this principle. When faced with a growth challenge, we didn't push harder. Instead, we stepped back, gathered in sacred space, and addressed the energetic imbalance that no business metric could measure but every attendee could feel.

This approach to strategic growth recognizes that business ecosystems, like natural ones, require periodic restoration of balance before new growth can emerge. Just as forests need occasional fires to clear underbrush and stimulate new life, businesses sometimes require energetic clearing to remove accumulated patterns that block authentic expansion. Would you learn that at Harvard?

Consider another client—a powerful healer and witch who was getting frustrated about bringing in women interested in her weekend program. They signed up and didn't show up. Didn't pay when due. She wanted to create a powerful and creative women's group, just not getting the energy. I saw what was needed and what needed to go away. In that hour, we turned it upside down, and within 60 days, she had her excited and committed group. In that meeting, I trusted my Imagination, Intention, Instinct, and Intuition, all driven by my power animal. And that breakthrough has moved her down her path, and her growth is moving forward.

In balancing your business between traditional process and awakening to your company's Spirit, you bring in a natural collaboration and community among your employees as well as with other women in business, as the potential of being a competitor drops off.

The strategic growth pillar of Sacred Shamanic Business Integration asks: What energetic patterns—within you, your team, or your business ecosystem—might be blocking your next level of expansion? What conventional growth strategies might you need to temporarily release to address these deeper patterns?

Reflection #3: *Where in your business do you feel resistance to growth, despite doing everything "right," according to conventional wisdom? What energetic patterns might need clearing before your next expansion can occur? What step backward might truly propel you forward?*

Value Creation: From Quantum Alignment to Team Empowerment

Value creation represents the third pillar of entrepreneurial success, yet most business approaches limit this concept to product features, service delivery, or customer experience. If you open up to the Spirit of your business, you will find the best way to go. It will likely expand your understanding of value to include energetic resonance—that is felt or sensed by your employees and flows in ripples through clients when they engage with your business.

Quantum Alignment for Distinctive Value

Your Quantum Self—that expansive consciousness that exists beyond time and personality—perceives value creation from a more profound perspective than quarterly projections or market trends. When you align with this expanded awareness, you naturally create offerings that resonate at frequencies your competitors can't access because these offerings emerge from your unique energetic signature.

That aspect of your business that is the Spirit or the aspect within you and possibly many employees and even clients that has a love of connection to the health of our earth. These elements have become more and more apparent in the world of business and marketing.

Consider bringing a ceremony into your business family. Odd maybe, but the shift of the energy is unique. In our work with women entrepreneurs, we find that it may be very stressful and that it cuts back on business and making deadlines. And yet there are several paths to clear the stress using nature and or creating ceremonies for the employees. A ceremony celebrating a breakthrough or a contract is magic. Think back to all the key moments in your life that you never acknowledged, much less celebrated.

Value what you create. Value those who help to create it. A ceremony for a department or the people in the office who were always there. And those that want what you have created will be able to feel the energy shift and know it is what they want!

These brief ceremonies honor ancient wisdom while fitting seamlessly into modern business contexts—bringing timeless practices into today's entrepreneurial challenges.

Reflection #4: *How might implementing energy-focused practices shift your team's creative capacity? What value remains uncreated because of energetic blocks within your organization? How might aligning with your Quantum Self reveal offerings that transcend market trends?*

Conclusion: Integrating the Sacred Into Your Bold Business Moves

Sacred Shamanic Business Integration offers a revolutionary approach to entrepreneurship—one that honors both ancient wisdom and modern business demands. By recognizing your business as a spiritual entity, accessing multidimensional guidance for decision-making, clearing energetic blocks to growth, and creating value through quantum alignment and team empowerment, you unlock an entirely new level of entrepreneurial power.

The boldest business moves rarely come from pushing harder along conventional paths but from aligning more deeply with the unseen energetic currents that influence all outcomes. As you continue your entrepreneurial journey, remember that you navigate not just one path but many—business leader, visionary, nurturer, and keeper of ancient wisdom. Your ability to integrate these aspects creates your unique power in the marketplace.

The women entrepreneurs who will thrive in tomorrow's business landscape won't be those who simply master conventional strategies but those who integrate those strategies with deeper wisdom, creating businesses that don't just succeed by external metrics but flourish as expressions of authentic purpose.

As we conclude this exploration of Sacred Shamanic Business Integration, I invite you to consider how these approaches might transform your next bold business move. Perhaps like my experience on that Las Vegas rooftop, you'll discover that the most powerful solution to your current challenge lies not in pushing harder but in gathering your courage to try something entirely different—something that honors the unseen dimensions of your business as much as the visible ones.

Final Reflection: *Having journeyed through this chapter, return to our opening question: Who are you? How has your understanding of yourself as an entrepreneur expanded or shifted? What bold business move is now calling to you from this place of integrated wisdom?*

Who Are You

Dr. Nefertiti S Fisher

Beautiful One Inc.
Teacher, Trainer, & Coach

https://www.linkedin.com/in/nefertitifisher/
https://www.facebook.com/profile.php?id=100000168393655
https://www.instagram.com/icome2inspireu/
https://www.bohcinc.com/
https://www.tiktok.com/@icome2inspireu?lang=en

Dr. Nefertiti is a John Maxwell Team certified speaker, teacher, trainer, and coach. She is passionate about personal development in all its forms, but her specialties are teaching and training. Dr. Nefertiti is also an Amazon Best Selling Author with three books on her shelf with more to come. As a certified teacher and trainer with the John Maxwell Team, not only is she equipped with a host of top-tier development resources to share with you but she has also been taught and trained by one of the world's foremost leadership experts, Dr. John C. Maxwell. John Maxwell has been an authority on leadership for more than 40 years, and if he's taught me anything, it's that teaching is ultimately serving. She is here to provide you with the tools you use to multiply your results; She is here to help you grow yourself, your team, and your organization beyond your barriers... and that is why I love what I do.

The Business Vision Is Yours

By Dr. Nefertiti S Fisher

In the realm of entrepreneurship and business development, few concepts are as powerful and personal as a business vision. It is the guiding star that illuminates the path for a company, offering direction and purpose to its endeavors. While financial metrics, strategic plans, and operational efficiencies are critical components of business success, none hold the same emotional weight or potential for inspiration as a well-crafted vision. The beauty and challenge of a business vision lie in the fact that it is uniquely yours. It reflects your values, aspirations, and dreams—a living testament to what you hope to achieve and how you wish to impact the world.

Defining a Business Vision

A business vision is a compelling picture of an organization's future. It answers the question: "What do we aspire to become?" Unlike a mission statement, which focuses on the present and outlines the organization's purpose, a vision is forward-looking. It is a dream made tangible, a beacon that both guides and motivates.

Key Characteristics of a Business Vision

1. **Inspirational**: A vision should ignite passion and enthusiasm. It should stir emotions and inspire commitment within the organization and beyond.
2. **Aspirational**: While grounded in reality, a vision should stretch the boundaries of what seems possible. It should push the organization toward growth and innovation.
3. **Clear and Concise**: Simplicity is key. A vision should be easily understood and remembered. It must convey its essence in a way that resonates with everyone in the organization.

4. **Future-Oriented**: It should provide a long-term perspective, setting sights on what the organization aims to achieve in the years to come.
5. **Unique**: Reflecting the individuality of its creator, a vision should set the organization apart from competitors, emphasizing its distinct values and goals.

Crafting Your Unique Vision

Creating a business vision is an introspective process, requiring deep reflection and understanding of one's core beliefs and ambitions. Here are some steps to help you shape your unique business vision:

1. Reflect on Personal Values and Beliefs

At the heart of every business vision are the values and beliefs of its creator. Consider what matters most to you both personally and professionally. Are there causes you are passionate about or principles you hold dear? Understanding these values will help ensure that your vision is authentic and deeply connected to who you are. No one else has the vision that was given to you, no matter how familiar it may look to someone else. Did Burger King care that there was a McDonald's? No, because their vision was similar and yet different. They both sell hamburgers.

2. Identify Core Competencies

Assess your organization's strengths and capabilities. What do you do better than anyone else? What unique skills or resources do you possess? A successful vision should leverage these strengths, using them as a foundation for future growth. Stay your true self when you are going through this phase because no one can do you like you, and remember that when you are building your vision, people around you will want you to change or be something you're not, and you! Don't let your own negative chatter tell you that you have to do it like someone else, you capitalize on your strengths and your abilities to be successful at what you do.

3. Understand Industry Trends

While a vision should be personal, it should also be informed by the realities of the industry. Stay informed about current trends, challenges, and opportunities. This knowledge will help you craft a vision that is both ambitious and achievable. You can never get antiquated in these times; technology is here, so embrace it for the benefit of your business. Always be willing to learn new things that will elevate your business.

4. Envision the Desired Impact

Consider the legacy you wish to leave. How do you want your organization to impact society, your industry, or the environment? A powerful vision often includes a social or environmental dimension, emphasizing the broader impact beyond financial success.

5. Articulate the Vision

With these insights, articulate your vision in a clear and compelling way. Use vivid language to paint a picture of the future. Ensure that it resonates not only with you but also with your team, customers, and stakeholders. This is so important and will make or break your vision. You have to be clear and concise because you will need runners to read your vision and assist you to the

next level, but you must be clear on your vision. This is not where you start getting shaky or wavering, you must be steadfast about your vision and a good steward of your vision as well.

Overcoming Challenges in Vision Creation

Creating a business vision is not without its challenges. It requires courage, introspection, and a willingness to embrace uncertainty. Here are some common obstacles and strategies to overcome them:

Fear of Failure

The fear of setting an ambitious vision and not achieving it can be paralyzing. However, remember that a vision is not a promise or a guarantee; it is a guiding light. Embrace the possibility of failure as a learning opportunity and a chance to refine and adapt your vision. So be okay with failure, it will make you stronger, and it will give you the opportunity to keep what didn't work and to learn from it to improve what did work. There is nothing wrong with setbacks and failures if you learn from them. Don't be afraid, this part will depict if you get back up again if you fail, and I am telling you, fall, dust yourself off, and get back to it! Why? Your vision depends on you.

Balancing Realism with Ambition

Finding the right balance between realism and ambition is crucial. A vision that is too realistic may lack inspiration, while one that is overly ambitious may seem unattainable. Seek feedback from trusted advisors and stakeholders to help strike this balance.

Aligning the Team

A vision is only as powerful as the people who believe in it. Ensuring that your team is aligned with and committed to the vision is essential. Communicate the vision clearly and consistently and encourage input and ownership from all levels of the organization.

The Role of Vision in Business Success

A strong business vision can be a catalyst for success, influencing various aspects of an organization, it's almost like your why, but for the business. You will have to remember this when times get challenging, when you are pressed, when you just want to give up, you must let your vision (why) fuel you to push past any obstacles.

Strategic Direction

A vision provides a framework for strategic decision-making. It helps prioritize initiatives, allocate resources, and guide long-term planning. By aligning strategies with the vision, organizations can stay focused on their ultimate goals.

Organizational Culture

A vision shapes the culture of an organization by defining its values and guiding principles. It influences how employees interact with one another, make decisions, and approach their work. A shared vision fosters a sense of unity and purpose, driving collaboration and innovation.

Customer Engagement

Customers are drawn to businesses that stand for something beyond profit. A compelling vision can enhance brand loyalty and customer engagement, as people connect emotionally with the organization's goals and values.

Attracting Talent

In a competitive job market, top talent seeks more than just a paycheck. They want to be part of something meaningful. A powerful vision can attract individuals who are aligned with the organization's values and who are eager to contribute to its success.

Vision in Practice: Examples from Leading Organizations

Several leading organizations have demonstrated the power of a compelling vision: Tesla: "To accelerate the world's transition to sustainable energy."

Tesla's vision reflects its commitment to sustainability and innovation. It is aspirational yet achievable, inspiring both employees and customers to support its mission of transforming the energy landscape.

Google: "To organize the world's information and make it universally accessible and useful."

Google's vision underscores its dedication to accessibility and utility. It encapsulates the company's core competencies in information technology and continues to guide its strategic initiatives.

Patagonia: "We're in business to save our home planet."

Patagonia's vision emphasizes environmental responsibility, reflecting the company's values and influencing its business practices. It inspires both employees and customers to support its mission of environmental stewardship.

The Evolution of a Vision

A business vision is not static; it evolves with the organization and the world around it. As external conditions change and new opportunities arise, a vision may need to be revisited and refined. This evolution is a natural part of the business journey and should be embraced as a chance to reaffirm commitment and adaptability.

Regular Review and Reflection

Schedule regular intervals to review the vision and assess its relevance. Gather feedback from stakeholders and consider the changing landscape. This reflection allows for recalibration and ensures that the vision remains aligned with the organization's direction and aspirations.

Communicating Changes

If adjustments to the vision are necessary, communicate them clearly and transparently. Explain the reasons behind the changes and how they will benefit the organization and its stakeholders. This transparency builds trust and reinforces commitment to the vision.

Conclusion: The Power of Your Unique Vision

In the end, the power of a business vision lies in its ability to inspire and guide. It is a personal declaration of what you hope to achieve and the impact you wish to have on the world. Embrace the responsibility and privilege of crafting your unique vision. Let it be the foundation upon which you build your business, and let it inspire others to join you on your journey. Remember, the business vision is yours only, and it holds the potential to transform not only your organization but the world around you.

NURTURE YOUR VISION, WORK YOUR VISION, AND PROTECT YOUR VISION!

Kayshaun Brooks

Founder of Renew You Body Butters

http://linkedin.com/in/kayshaun-brooks-bb858416b
https://www.facebook.com/kayshaun.brookscrosby
https://www.instagram.com/therealkayshaunbrooks
https://www.renewyoubodybutter.com/
https://linktr.ee/renewyoubodybutters

Kayshaun Brooks is a World Record Holder, a former nurse, and Holistic Pain & Trauma Warrior. She is the owner of the 3x award-winning holistic skincare company, Renew You Body Butters. Specializing in sensitive skin issues like eczema, rosacea, and hyperpigmentation. Her company offers wholesale and private label services. Kayshaun has partnered with over 60 affiliates and 1 celebrity brand ambassador to promote her products. She also helps entrepreneurs launch and scale their own affiliate programs, focusing on collaboration and relationship building.

The Power of Collaboration & Affiliate Marketing in Business

By Kayshaun Brooks

For twenty years, I dedicated my life to the medical field, pouring my energy into caring for others. My days were filled with patient interactions, where I witnessed the transformative power of health and wellness. However, my career took an unexpected turn when I was severely injured while working at a prison. The physical and emotional toll of that experience forced me to leave the medical profession, plunging me into a world of chronic illness that left me bedridden. Yet, within this challenging period, I found the spark to embark on a new journey: creating my holistic skincare company.

As I navigated the complexities of my health, I realized that the skills I honed in medicine, empathy, resilience, and strategic thinking would be essential as I ventured into entrepreneurship. The boldest move I made was not just launching a skincare line but developing an innovative affiliate marketing program centered on networking, collaboration, and building meaningful relationships. This approach not only empowered others but also sustained my business in a way that aligned with my values.

The Turning Point

Long before my injury, I had been crafting skincare products for nearly a decade. This passion began as a personal quest to find natural solutions for my skin issues and for my children. My hands-on experience informed my vision for a skincare line that emphasized natural ingredients and self-care, rooted in the same principles of healing I once practiced in medicine and holistic wellness.

The injury I sustained at the prison was a pivotal moment in my life. It forced me to reevaluate my career and my identity. The pain from the injuries was overwhelming, and soon after, I began experiencing chronic illness symptoms that left me bedridden. What felt like an insurmountable obstacle became the catalyst that ignited my entrepreneurial spirit.

During this tumultuous time, I reflected on my experiences in healthcare and my passion for holistic wellness. I had always been a "product of the product," and my desire to create effective skincare solutions led me to customize products for myself and others. This rich background fueled my determination to launch a skincare line that could help others heal, even as I faced my own challenges. I learned in a functional pain course I was taking that helping others heal was helping manage my chronic pain mentally.

Building an Affiliate Marketing Program Through Collaboration

While bedridden, I began researching how to launch my skincare line and started working with a business consultant. One of the most significant challenges was figuring out how to market my products effectively without being able to engage in traditional hands-on methods, and the lack of resources and finances. It was during this reflection that I recognized the importance of community and connection in business. I wanted my affiliate marketing program to be more than just a sales strategy; it needed to foster genuine relationships among individuals who shared a passion for holistic health.

The idea of creating a collaborative affiliate program blossomed after two individuals approached me in the same week, expressing their love for my products and my story. They both asked how they could become affiliates. I asked my mentor what an affiliate was and what these ladies were asking me for. I was informed this would be like my own referral program. Or I could look at it like I would be forming a holistic Mary Kay or a holistic Avon. I have had my share of working for network marketing companies. I have had good and bad experiences. I told myself if I did this, I'm not doing those tactics that those other companies did. I wanted to be different.

I realized the potential for a network built on support and shared values. Inspired by their enthusiasm, I envisioned a program where affiliates would not only promote my products but also support each other, share insights, and celebrate successes together. This community-oriented approach would create a positive environment where everyone could thrive.

I started outlining the structure of my affiliate program with these principles in mind. Accessibility and reward were key components. I wanted to ensure that anyone interested could join, regardless of their background or experience, but we have to be in alignment with one another. By focusing on collaboration rather than competition, I aimed to cultivate a supportive network of advocates who genuinely believed in my products and the mission behind my brand. This is where making it mandatory to use my company Renew You Body Butters' holistic skincare products. I'm a product of the products, and so will each and every affiliate.

To kick off the program, I started sharing with some people about my vision, and they loved it, wanted to support me, and those who shared my vision. These were not just potential affiliates; they were partners in a shared journey toward promoting holistic health. Together, we formed a community dedicated to uplifting one another while championing the benefits of natural skincare. Within the first five months, I had fifteen affiliates and one celebrity brand ambassador.

Developing Meaningful Relationships

As I launched the affiliate marketing program, I prioritized building relationships over transactions. I understood that successful marketing is rooted in trust and authenticity. I met with each affiliate to introduce myself and share my vision for the program. These meetings provided a platform for affiliates to connect with me, share their experiences, and discuss how we could best support one another.

During these sessions, I encouraged open dialogue. I let them know this is not my affiliate marketing program, it's *our* affiliate marketing program. I wanted my affiliates to feel comfortable sharing their thoughts, ideas, and even their challenges. By fostering an atmosphere of collaboration, I aimed to create a sense of belonging and camaraderie. This approach not only strengthened our connections but also sparked creativity and innovation within the group.

As we discussed strategies and shared feedback, I realized that my affiliates brought diverse perspectives that enriched my brand's messaging. They were not just promoting products; they were sharing stories that resonated with their audiences. This authenticity helped forge deeper connections with potential customers, as they could see the genuine passion behind the promotion.

Overcoming Challenges Together

Building this collaborative affiliate marketing program was not without its challenges. Managing logistics from my bed requires meticulous organization and a great deal of creativity. I relied heavily on digital tools and platforms to streamline communication and collaboration with my affiliates.

Recruiting affiliates proved to be another learning curve. It was essential to build trust and demonstrate the value of my skincare products while sharing my personal story. Many potential affiliates resonated with my journey, which helped them connect more deeply with my brand. I found that vulnerability was a powerful tool in creating relationships. People were inspired by my story and motivated to share it.

As the program began to grow, I made it a priority to engage with my affiliates regularly. I offered support, celebrated their successes, and encouraged them to share their journeys. The sense of community we created became crucial; I wanted my affiliates to feel like they were part of something bigger than just a marketing program.

I hosted virtual webinars where we could dive deeper into marketing strategies, product knowledge, and personal development. These sessions not only educated my affiliates but also strengthened our bonds. We shared our wins and challenges, creating a safe space where everyone felt valued and heard.

Falling in Love with My Affiliate Marketing Program

After a year of running my affiliate marketing program, I was personally invited to the White Label World Expo in Las Vegas. I was so scared to do this event. Only because I knew I was potentially facing cancer and had to have surgery to remove some tumors. This event would be only a few short months after the surgery, and I would still be recovering. Also, this would be one of the biggest business risks I would be taking.

I knew my kids and I could not do this event alone. I was casually mentioning the opportunity to my affiliates, wishing we knew each other in person and not just virtually. Some of them said, "What does that have to do with anything?" Long story short, several of my affiliates flew across the United States to come help and work at this expo representing my company, Renew You Body Butters. To keep it real with y'all, I didn't pay for flights, hotel rooms, or food. Not because I didn't want to, but because I couldn't. This event was costing me close to $10,000, and I didn't have another dollar to spare. Moving in faith, we came and conquered the event. We made such an incredible impression at the expo that businesses were trying to buy my company from me on day 2. We went in there and the whole building knew who Renew You Body Butters was. This experience showed me the power of networking, collaborating, and building relationships in an affiliate marketing program.

Achievements Through Collaboration

As our collaborative affiliate marketing program gained traction, I witnessed the fruits of our collective efforts. Sales began to rise, and I was able to invest in expanding my product line. My affiliates transformed from mere promoters into passionate brand ambassadors, sharing their own testimonials and creating authentic connections with their audiences.

The recognition of my skincare company receiving three prestigious awards was not just a personal triumph; it was a testament to the power of community-driven marketing. I realized that my affiliate program was more than a revenue-generating strategy; it was a platform for others to build their own businesses while advocating for holistic health. I have had affiliations start their own skincare product lines, their own hair care lines, and more. My affiliates are partially what led my business to do private labeling and wholesale.

Each success story from my affiliates reaffirmed my belief in the mission behind my brand. Their journeys mirrored my own, and together, we were breaking boundaries in the beauty industry. It was incredibly rewarding to see women empowering themselves through our collaboration. Their growth became a reflection of our collective commitment to holistic wellness and authentic marketing.

Lessons Learned from Collaboration

Through this experience, I learned critical lessons about entrepreneurship and the importance of collaboration. First, I understood that building a successful business often hinges on leveraging the strengths of others. My affiliates brought diverse perspectives and creativity that enriched my brand's messaging.

Moreover, I discovered that strategic risk-taking can lead to unexpected rewards. Launching an affiliate program centered around collaboration while dealing with my health challenges was daunting, but it opened new avenues for growth and community engagement. It reinforced my belief that true innovation often arises from adversity.

Finally, I learned the power of authenticity in marketing. By sharing my story and inviting others to do the same, we created a genuine connection with our customers. This authenticity resonated in our branding and communication, fostering loyalty and trust.

Conclusion

Building my luxury holistic skincare brand Renew You Body Butters and launching my affiliate marketing program from the ground up has been nothing short of a powerful journey, one that wouldn't have been possible without God, and without the unwavering support of my mentor and friend, Tiffany Mason. Tiffany is an exceptional business consultant who challenged me, guided me, and inspired me to make bold, strategic moves that transformed my vision into reality.

Reflecting on my journey from the medical field to launching a holistic skincare company, I am filled with gratitude for the struggles that shaped my path. The affiliate marketing program I developed not only became a cornerstone of my business but also empowered others to embark on their own entrepreneurial journey. I have coined myself as the modern-day Madam CJ Walker. She was the first Black self-made millionaire in the early 1900s. She had over ten thousand sales associates (affiliates). My goal is to surpass this number and make just as big of an impact as she has made in history. To every person reading this, I encourage you to embrace your unique story and consider the innovative paths available to you. Whether through affiliate marketing or another avenue, your bold business moves can create a ripple effect of change and opportunity. Remember, resilience in the face of challenges can lead to remarkable growth both personally and professionally. Together, let's celebrate our stories and support one another in our pursuits. The journey may be challenging, but the connections we build along the way will make all the difference.

Kimberly Tyler

https://www.linkedin.com/in/kimberly-tyler-a8849539/
https://www.facebook.com/profile.php?id=100094747320115
https://www.instagram.com/brokenvesselholylight
https://www.brokenvesselholylight.com/

Kimberly Tyler, M.Ed, is an international best-selling author with over 30 years of experience in education and children's ministry leadership. A retired educational administrator, she possesses a wealth of knowledge and experience in student success through positive learning environments and advocacy of inclusive practices. Kimberly is an inspiring author with a profound gift for seeing others succeed despite any challenges that they may face. Residing in Northern California on an urban homestead with her husband and extended family, she draws inspiration from the beautiful surroundings and close-knit community. Kimberly's writing reflects her genuine desire to uplift and empower readers as she shares stories that resonate with faith, hope, and resilience. Her unique blend of storytelling and encouragement has positively impacted the hearts of readers worldwide. An accomplished creative, her favorite mediums are fabric arts such as quilting and embroidery. She can be found on her Facebook page Brokenvesselholylight, and at
http://www.brokenvesselholylight.com

Embracing the Mindset of an Authorpreneur

By Kimberly Tyler

Starting any new journey is never easy, especially when it comes to entrepreneurship in writing and publishing or authorpreneurship. It takes remarkable courage to dream of becoming an author and even more to take that first step. When you decide to share your story and voice with the world, you face and must overcome the uncertainty, fear of rejection, and worry that no one will care about your message. But here's the truth: the only way to become an author is to start, and the only way to get your message out is to join the conversation. For many of us, that first shaky but determined step is the real victory of that journey. When I accepted an invitation to collaborate on my first book project, the doubts were deafening. "What if no one reads it? What if no one likes it? What if I fail?" But a quieter voice inside me whispered, "What if this is the beginning of something bigger than you can imagine? What if this is your next step?" That whisper was enough.

I have found that this journey is all about boldness—having the courage and willingness to take risks, push through the challenges, and create something of lasting value. For many aspiring authors, writing the book feels like the biggest hurdle. In some ways, it is. Pouring your heart and soul onto the page, crafting something meaningful, and pushing through self-doubt is no small feat. Whether you're just starting out or feeling stuck in your creative process, remember that every successful entrepreneur, published author, and thriving artist once stood where you are, staring down your fears and choosing the less traveled path, but remember it is a rewarding path.

Do not Despise Small Beginnings.

One of the greatest lessons I learned early on was the power of saying "yes" to opportunities—even when I felt unprepared. My journey began with small steps, taking on writing opportunities that stretched me and co-authoring books that pushed me beyond my comfort zone. When invited to contribute to a bestselling international book platform, I hesitated, doubting whether my voice belonged. But I said yes, and in doing so, I learned that confidence doesn't come before action—it comes through action, and the more you step out, the easier the next step comes. Writing is more about impact than making money. It's about reaching people with your story and message, showing up, writing through the doubts, and trusting that your words and voice matter.

Being an author isn't about perfection. It's about courage—the courage to start, keep going and embrace the highs and hard lessons along the way. When you take that first step, you might discover that writing a book isn't only about what you give to the world—it's also about who you become in the process.

The Business of Writing

Seeing a book with your picture, name, and best-seller statistics is incredible. Still, while seeing my name on book covers and celebrating success was fantastic, I quickly realized that publishing a book was just one of the many next steps. Many authors don't realize until they publish that writing is only half the battle. We have written, edited, and gone through all the publishing steps only to find the real challenge begins after the book is written. Marketing, sales, and audience engagement matter as much—if not more—than the words themselves. Because no matter how good a book is, if no one knows about it, it won't sell. I learned this the hard way. I assumed that if I wrote a great book with a great publisher, readers would naturally find it. But I quickly realized that this is not the case. Authors must also be marketers, strategists, and business-minded creatives. Social media, email lists, speaking engagements, and collaborations all play a role in getting a book into the hands of readers. It's not enough to write—you have to promote, connect, and consistently show up.

Many authors struggle with monetization, assuming that book royalties alone will sustain them. The truth is that royalties fluctuate, and competition is fierce. That's why successful authors often diversify their income streams—offering courses, coaching, speaking engagements, or other creative business ventures tied to their books. Everything changed when I accepted that I needed to stop seeing myself as "just an author" and embraced the mindset of an authorpreneur. I wasn't just writing books—I was building a brand, creating a community, and positioning my work for long-term impact. Instead of waiting for opportunities, I learned to make them. Instead of hoping readers would find me, I found ways to reach them. The shift from seeing writing as a passion to treating it as a business was the game-changer that turned my books into something more than just words on a page—it turned them into a platform for real influence and sustainability.

Building a Brand and Community

The authorpreneur's journey is filled with highs and lows, victories and setbacks, moments of clarity, and seasons of uncertainty. Critical to success in this journey is building a business brand and community. This is the key for anyone stepping into the publishing world: Writing is the foundation, but business keeps it standing. If you want to thrive as an author, you must embrace both because becoming an author isn't just about writing—it's about being seen. And that means stepping into the often uncomfortable world of marketing and entrepreneurship. For many writers, including myself, this shift doesn't come naturally. I wanted to write, not sell. I wanted to share my story, not figure out reports, algorithms, and engagement strategies. However, I had to embrace the learning curve of building a brand if I wanted my work to reach people.

One of the first steps I took was creating a Facebook page, an Instagram account, and a website. It felt strange at first—putting myself out there, announcing my work to the world. I wasn't even sure what to post. Would people care? Would they judge me? But I realized that if I didn't take control of my brand, no one else would. These platforms weren't just about selling books; they were about connection, about creating a space where readers could find me, engage with my message, and journey with me. But self-promotion wasn't easy. I worried about being too pushy or sounding like I was trying to sell something. The truth is that many authors feel this discomfort, but the key to overcoming it is shifting perspective. Promotion isn't about bragging—it's about serving. It's about sharing your work with people who need it and who will benefit from your words. The more I focused on who I was helping rather than how I felt, the easier it became. Keeping my focus on my true purpose of writing enabled me to push forward and put in the time needed to build my platform. I knew my purpose in writing was to encourage, equip, and empower, and when I accepted this was an extension of that, it became easier.

Trial and error became my most outstanding teacher in social media marketing. Some posts resonated, while others flopped. I learned the importance of consistency, authenticity, and storytelling—people connect with people, not just products. I discovered that engagement mattered more than numbers and that building trust was more valuable than going viral. Being consistent and present was my most valuable asset, not having perfect social posts and content. I found if you're willing to put yourself out there, learn, and adjust along the way, you'll find that your brand isn't just about marketing—it's about building a community around your message.

Embracing Learning and Growth Seasons

My journey of moving from a passive mindset to an active one required me to invest in my learning and growth by taking courses on marketing, joining mentorship programs, and reading everything I could about branding, audience engagement, and business strategy. This investment wasn't just about growing my skills—it was about shifting my mindset from seeing myself as just a writer to seeing myself as a business owner. I knew these new skills would allow me to drive sales, create opportunities, and build a lasting presence in my industry.

Another critical lesson was the power of relationships. Building a brand isn't a solo journey. Networking with the right people—fellow authors, business owners, and mentors—opened doors I never could have accessed alone. Collaboration, support, and learning from others greatly impacted my growth. Whether through online communities, masterminds, or in-person events, I discovered that the right relationships could accelerate progress in ways I never imagined. But growth didn't come without setbacks. There were months when my learning curve was slow and countless frustrating moments when tech issues made everything feel impossible. I had to learn to pivot, adapt, and see challenges as stepping stones and opportunities rather than roadblocks. Every setback forced me to improve—to rethink my strategies, refine my messaging, and get more creative in how I connected with my audience. Instead of seeing struggles as failures, I began to see them as part of the journey.

Creating Lasting Impact

Reflecting on our discussion in this chapter, we see that authorpreneurship isn't about figuring it all out from the start. It's about being bold enough to be willing to learn and grow to reach those we seek to serve. True success in authorpreneurship isn't just about making money—it's about making an impact. Your influence measures true success, the lives you touch, and the value you bring to others. If you focus solely on numbers, you'll constantly chase the next sale. But if you focus on impact, the sales will follow, and more importantly, your work will have lasting meaning. The ultimate goal isn't just to sell a product—it's to create something meaningful that continues to add value over time. When you shift your focus from making sales to making an impact, you'll grow your business and build a legacy far beyond yourself. Writing is more than just a creative outlet—it's a tool for transformation. A book can be the foundation of a business, a message that sparks change, and a vehicle for teaching and inspiring others. Many successful authors don't just stop at publishing books; they use their words as a springboard to build something more significant. Writing opens the door to a broader platform that allows you to reach and serve more people. Instead of relying solely on book sales, successful writers find ways to expand their reach. Speaking engagements provide opportunities to connect with audiences in real-time, courses allow more profound teaching, coaching offers personal transformation, and digital products like workbooks, guides, and memberships create passive income streams. The key is recognizing that your knowledge and experience have value beyond just the pages of your book. Long-term value in business comes from consistently showing up, offering solutions, and building trust. A single book might introduce someone to your work, but continued engagement keeps them returning. Providing high-quality content, fostering community, and always looking for ways to serve your audience ensures that your impact lasts beyond a one-time purchase. Successful brands aren't built overnight; they're built through dedication, generosity, and a commitment to making a positive difference for your audience. In teaching, we have a saying: "People don't care how much you know until they know how much you care." This is true of your audience.

Looking Ahead

Every journey has milestones, but growth doesn't stop once you reach a goal—it's about looking ahead and asking, "What's next?" The vision for the future is clear: more books, business expansion, and more significant impact. Writing is just the beginning. I see new projects, deeper connections with my audience, and a growing platform allowing me to serve more significantly. Whether launching new courses, expanding my brand, or stepping into new speaking opportunities, I know there is always room to stretch and evolve. But beyond my personal journey, my heart is set on encouraging other women entrepreneurs to take bold steps in their own paths. Too often, we let fear, doubt, or imposter syndrome keep us from stepping into the fullness of our calling. I want every woman who dreams of writing a book, starting a business, or building something meaningful to know this: You are capable. You are qualified. And the only thing standing between you and your success is the decision to begin. The road isn't always easy, but persistence and faith make all the difference. Every challenge, every season, and every moment of uncertainty shapes you for what's ahead. Trust that the process works in your favor, even when it doesn't feel like it.

The most successful authorpreneurs aren't the ones who had it all figured out from the start—they're the ones who kept showing up, refining their craft, and pushing forward despite setbacks. So here's my challenge to you: What bold business move will you make today? Will you finally start that book? Launch that business? Step out of your comfort zone and take action. Whatever it is, don't wait for the perfect time—the ideal time is now. Your dreams are valid, your voice matters, and your work has the power to create a lasting impact. The next chapter of your journey is waiting, but it won't write itself. It's time to step forward with courage, faith, and determination. Your future success awaits. You've come this far. You've read about the challenges, the victories, the lessons learned, and the risks taken. The question isn't "Can you do this?"—it's "Will you?" The truth is, no one is ever fully ready. No one wakes up one day with all the answers, the perfect plan, and an obstacle-free path to success. Every entrepreneur, every author, every business owner started right where you are—on the edge of a decision. The difference between those who succeed and those who don't isn't talent or luck; it's action. Success isn't built on one grand, life-changing moment. It's built on small, consistent, and courageous steps. It's showing up when you feel uncertain, taking risks even when doubt creeps in, and pushing forward despite setbacks. It's about embracing the journey—not just the destination—and trusting that every step you take, no matter how small, is moving you closer to your goals. You don't have to have it all figured out today. But you do have to start. Maybe your next step is writing that first chapter, launching your website, or contacting someone who can help guide you. Perhaps it's simply saying yes to the dream that's been stirring inside you for far too long. Whatever it is, take that step now. Keep learning. Keep growing. Keep taking risks. The road to success isn't straight or easy, but it is yours to walk. The world needs your ideas, your voice, and your boldness. Don't wait for the perfect time—the ideal time is now. So, I leave you with this: What bold business move will you make today? It's time to step forward in faith, take ownership of your journey, and build something that lasts. Your future is waiting. Go make it happen.

Maureen Byers

Maureen Byers GRI
Master of Real Estate & National Innovator

https://www.linkedin.com/in/maureen-b-63938997
https://www.facebook.com/share/1AxVaGqnER/
https://www.instagram.com/byersmaureen
https://wa.me/+18584137887

Maureen Byers is a pioneering force in Colorado, Arizona, and California real estate. Starting as a single mother relying on assistance, she transformed her life into that of a successful broker, investor, and entrepreneur. With an advanced education and extensive experience facilitating high-value real estate transactions, Maureen specializes in commercial investment, creative financing, and property development. As a 1031 tax-deferred exchanger and seller financing expert, she skillfully navigates complex transactions for a global clientele. Her entrepreneurial spirit led her to establish a brokerage where she has represented and supported aspiring real estate professionals. Maureen's approach combines hard work with innovative strategies she learned along her journey, allowing her to embrace her uniqueness and authenticity. She believes true achievement is not just measured by financial milestones but by the ability to inspire others and help them reach their goals. Today, Maureen leads a vibrant real estate investment network dedicated to empowering individuals in their pursuit of financial independence.

Building Bridges: The Power of Networking in Bold Business Moves

By Maureen Byers

Embracing the journey of entrepreneurship as a woman in a male-dominated industry has been both challenging and rewarding. My path as a seasoned Commercial Investment Real Estate Broker and Designated Multi-State Real Estate Broker has spanned nearly five decades. Known as "The Broker Broker," I take pride in delivering exceptional value and reliability to my clients while forging lasting relationships. This journey has not only been about business; it has been a testament to the power of perseverance, creativity, and faith.

In today's real estate market, we find ourselves in a unique situation, often described as a perfect storm for investors. Timing is crucial, and I firmly believe that now is the moment to act. The phrase, "It's easier to give birth than it is to raise the dead," resonates deeply with me, emphasizing the importance of seizing opportunities while they are ripe. The current landscape presents diverse prospects, especially in areas such as foreclosures and creative financing. As women, we possess a unique ability to approach challenges through collaboration, nurturing relationships, and empowering one another, which sets us apart in this industry.

My venture into real estate began with a bold decision to step into a field that many perceive as daunting, particularly for women. I faced numerous obstacles and skepticism, yet my unwavering belief in my capabilities fueled my perseverance. Throughout my career, I have come to understand that success is not merely about knowledge; it is rooted in resilience, adaptability, and the willingness to take calculated risks.

Working alongside my dedicated team, including Kurtis Clay, an invaluable Institutional Consultant, we bring a cumulative 86 years of experience in real estate investing. My specialization in real estate and liquidations ensures that I can facilitate smooth transactions while maximizing client value. Kurtis's expertise in matching properties to specific investment criteria enhances our effectiveness, allowing us to identify and develop lucrative opportunities in a rapidly changing market. Together, we share a collective passion for flipping properties, infusing fresh perspectives and innovative strategies into our projects.

Collaboration is not just beneficial; it is essential in this industry. Relying solely on individual expertise can limit our potential. I have learned the importance of surrounding myself with talented individuals who complement my skills and share my vision. This collaborative approach, strengthened by Kurtis's insights and connections, has led to successful outcomes and has enriched my understanding of the market dynamics.

In every transaction, I emphasize professionalism and transparency. Key documentation, such as a Real Estate Associate Consultant (REAC) firm and Non-Disclosure Agreements (NDAs), ensures confidentiality and protects the interests of all parties involved. Establishing clear expectations and maintaining open lines of communication creates a foundation of trust that is vital for long-term success.

Health, I believe, is our true wealth. This year, I partnered with Julie Park, a health and wellness expert dedicated to holistic well-being rather than just weight loss. I am particularly excited to introduce Body Balance, featuring hormonal drops and a low insulin diet that have positively impacted my life. This initiative reflects my belief that personal well-being is integral to professional success. If we do not prioritize our health, pursuing our ambitions becomes increasingly challenging.

Incorporating wellness into my daily routine has transformed my approach to business. I prioritize self-care, recognizing that a healthy mind and body are critical to navigating the demands of entrepreneurship. As women, we often juggle multiple responsibilities, and it is essential to carve out time for ourselves to recharge and refocus.

Our property selection process is meticulous. We handpick and match properties to clients' criteria, utilizing an extensive database to conduct thorough searches across various areas and cities. After signing an NDA, clients specify their preferences regarding location, property type, and price range. This tailored approach ensures we find the best opportunities aligned with their investment goals.

I believe that every client deserves personalized attention and care. By understanding their unique needs and aspirations, I can guide them toward properties that resonate with their vision. This client-centric philosophy has been a cornerstone of my success in the industry.

My current focus is on nationwide foreclosures and creative solutions for income-producing properties, particularly in regions like Florida, Texas, the Carolinas, Arizona, Colorado, and California. I hold licenses in Colorado, Arizona, and California, with previous licenses in New Mexico and Illinois. I am actively exploring expansions into Nevada, Georgia, Texas, and Florida.

This diverse market focus allows me to adapt to changing trends and capitalize on emerging opportunities. As I expand my reach, I remain committed to providing clients with the highest level of service and expertise. The real estate landscape is ever-evolving, and staying ahead of the curve is essential.

My areas of expertise include broker investment, where I identify lucrative opportunities across various property types, creative financing techniques such as seller financing and 1031 tax-deferred exchanges, and my passion for flipping properties, new construction, and resort properties. I also work on developing and selling vacant land, managing the liquidation process for properties, and I am open to consulting opportunities, ghostwriting, and partnerships.

Currently, I am selecting twelve investors for mentorship partnerships over the next twelve months, and we are nearing capacity. This initiative is open to serious investors, whether novices or experts, who are interested in collaborating on small lucrative partnerships and innovative projects. Mentorship is a powerful tool for growth and development. I believe in fostering relationships that empower others to reach their full potential. By sharing my experiences and insights, I aim to equip aspiring investors with the knowledge and confidence necessary to navigate the real estate landscape.

This year has been particularly rewarding as I proudly became a published author, contributing to a chapter of a New York and Amazon best-selling book that emphasizes the importance of investors, entrepreneurs, and empowering women in real estate. Writing has allowed me to share my journey and insights with a broader audience, inspiring others to pursue their dreams within the industry.

The act of writing is a reflection of my commitment to continuous learning and growth. By documenting my experiences, I not only share valuable lessons but also solidify my understanding of the concepts I discuss. It serves as a reminder that our stories possess the power to inspire and uplift others, making them feel connected and understood.

Faith plays a pivotal role in my business endeavors. I believe in the power of faith and the guidance of a higher power in our pursuits. My mission is to create significant value for my clients while cultivating connections that resonate with success and purpose. Faith serves as my anchor, providing me with the strength to overcome challenges and the clarity to pursue my goals.

In building relationships, I have learned the importance of authenticity and vulnerability. Sharing my experiences, both triumphs and struggles, fosters deeper connections with my clients and colleagues. We are all navigating our unique paths, and by supporting one another, we create a community of empowerment.

As I reflect on my journey in the real estate industry, I am reminded of the challenges and victories that have shaped my path. My experiences have taught me that success is not a destination; rather, it is a continuous journey of growth, learning, and connection. I encourage women to embrace their entrepreneurial spirit, take bold steps toward their goals, and support one another in this pursuit.

The road to entrepreneurship may be paved with obstacles, but it is also filled with abundant opportunities for empowerment, collaboration, and success. Together, we can redefine what it means to be a woman in business, breaking down barriers and building a future where our voices are heard and valued.

For those interested in starting a brokerage, becoming a broker, or exploring partnerships in real estate or related industries, I encourage you to reach out. The path to entrepreneurship is not always easy, but it is incredibly rewarding. Together, we can navigate the landscape of real estate, sharing insights and experiences that empower us to succeed.

Are you ready to unlock your potential in real estate? I invite you to connect with me for a personal consultation. Let's discuss your goals, answer your questions, and explore how we can collaborate to achieve success together.

You can reach me, Maureen Byers, at 858-413-7887 or via email at oceansidemaureen@gmail.com. Together, let's make the coming years a remarkable chapter in our journeys, filled with HER BOLD BUSINESS MOVES.

Gracy Goldman

CEO of Suits & Saints Ltd

https://www.gracygoldman.com/
https://suitsandsaints.com/
support@suitsandsaints.com
https://www.instagram.com/gracy_goldman/
https://www.instagram.com/suitsandsaints/
https://www.linkedin.com/in/gracygoldman/

Gracy Goldman is a professional actress, soon to be appearing in both season one and season two of WEDNESDAY, directed by Tim Burton. She is also the founder of Suits & Saints Ltd, an organization dedicated to helping creatives—actors, artists, writers, and entrepreneurs—build sustainable careers driven by passion and purpose. Through strategic coaching and mentorship, she empowers individuals to break free from limiting structures, whether in traditional employment or the creative industries, and take control of their professional journeys. With firsthand experience navigating both the entertainment industry and entrepreneurship, she provides the tools and mindset shifts needed to scale creative ambitions into lasting success. Her book offers insight into risk-taking, growth strategies, and the power of self-agency, guiding creatives toward a future where artistic vision and financial independence go hand in hand.

The Dream Engineer Who Carved Her Own Path - A Light Worker's Guide to Dancing with Agency

By Gracy Goldman

When I was 23 years old, I had a near-death experience.

I guess, like death, no two *near-death* experiences are the same. For me, it was a bit like falling out of the sky and into the cosmos. 'Out of body' it most certainly was.

It seems fitting to start my journey here.

Looking back, I can only describe the force with which I re-entered my body as so intense it sent a blast of wind hurtling through my physical form and out my rectum at lightning speed, rudely awakening my friend Annette from deep slumbers. The stench burst through the room like shockwaves in the 100 GHz zone, so stinky it must have felt like a hundred elephants had just sat on her face all at once.

(She tells the tale better than me, I'm pretty sure it must have been an ordeal.)

"Phaaw! Phaw, phaw, phaw, phaw!!! ... " Annette, swishing round abruptly, her back away from me, clenching her nose. I, at this point, was still not really consciously back in my body, so her yelps sounded distant, remote. Like being in a bell jar underwater, and not fully comprehending the echoey sounds around me.

As for me, the whole experience left a mark in a totally different way. I was young and had been suffering a devastating heartache when I took off home to spend the Christmas holidays in Holland with my family. I had invited Annette along for the ride. Perhaps something already instinctively told me I didn't think I would make it on my own. The sadness was real. Palpable. It's been a long time since I've thought about it, yet I can still feel the tendrils from that long-ago past even now. It shaped me. Well, I guess everyone knows that first heartache feeling, but this blow had a poison tip to it and hit me harder and longer than any other human interaction I have ever had.

Still, the beauty I felt in that wondrously miasmic moment was also like nothing I had ever felt before. When I awoke from my cosmic travels, what I felt was exquisite, something so otherworldly it was hard to put into words. Just to say, that as Annette recovered from her suffering for a brief second, she too became suddenly arrested by my radiant auric field. The conversation went something like this:

"You. look. beautiful." Her eyes stared at me for a brief second.

"I know," I replied.

It came from an otherworldly place of 'knowingness,' there was no arrogance attached. Just a simplistic, pure sense of knowing. I had been someplace else. So, there it was. My rank rebirth back into life, filled with a profound depth of love, clarity, and radiance. I had been rescued from a black cloud shrouding me, the toxins had been dispelled, and I had gained re-entrance into the world of sunlight again.

The years that followed were pretty crazy for me. I was a relatively fresh graduate in acting at the time, having spent three years at the Royal Academy of Dramatic Art (RADA). Before my near-death experience, I was a young, hungry, ambitious starlet with big dreams, busting it into Hollywood. After my near-death experience, the love and passion for the work, which never left me, got stifled, strong-armed by crushing oversensitivity.

The city had become too big, intense, and overstimulating for me. Almost everything made me jump in London and for a while I even lost the power to express myself. I was changed. And the change was definitely generating an awkward trajectory for my acting career. I'd become introverted, *worse*, the tools an actor needs in their arsenal, the ability to play with words both on the page and in the imagination, both had temporarily abandoned me. Those who knew me as a daring, outgoing, bodacious individual were stumped at this noticeable transformation, and among them were those who seized the opportunity to take advantage.

The whole process, though, was preparing me for something so much bigger than I could ever imagine.

I became fascinated with esoteric teachings. I wanted to read more and more about the scientific studies of extraterrestrial, angelic, and otherworldly phenomena. I needed to comprehend some of what I had been through. These out-of-this-world experiences were real; I needed to find something I could confide in. For some reason, reading felt important. Digesting the sturdy convictions of people with established backgrounds who were of sound mind was the order of the day. There was no way I was going to be classified 'woo-woo' or 'airy fairy', or worse, 'crazy'. Still, to be fair, I'd become so jittery and introverted I wasn't really that far off from any of those things.

It just needed to make sense. What was I experiencing and *why?*

I had questions, most of them unanswerable. I was having such watershed moments in my relationships, my sense of self, and above all, how to grapple with and keep hold of a career I loved so much that felt as if it was slipping away from me by the day. In every manner of expression, I was a shell of my former self. I felt like I was losing the very instrument I was born to play with. I was struggling to make ends meet, with one foot straddling the smokey echelons of London Town, and the other the cosmic fields of existence where, to be honest, I felt most at home; things were awkward to say the least.

I became excited by the various Laws of Mental Science. Back then, I came across Abraham Hicks, and the Law of Attraction, I studied *Meetings With Angels* by Dr H.C. Moolenburgh. A firsthand discussion from people with real-life encounters of the unknown. One of the first books I read, in fact. It was a book that fell off the bookshelf where I stood, asking to come home with me. To my utter amazement, so many of the people, places, and encounters Moollenburgh depicted in his work, I knew! The street names were not only familiar Dutch names, but the areas in some cases were places where I had grown up. I knew some of the long, windy lanes he was talking about. Confirmation, I was on the right track.

The more I studied, the stronger I got. I was still cagey with my communications, after all, I was studying quack stuff, and this made me feel too fragile to face certain mistrust or disbelief. Not when to me, it all seemed plain as day. I didn't want anyone to crush my spirits with rejection, so I kept this ever-growing side to me, locked away from public consumption.

As the knowledge I was gaining began to enhance my own life; the more I learned, the less I understood why we were not raised on these original imprints from birth. Why were we not taught these things in school? How to expand our true soul's blueprint, and begin from the heart of our true mission, passion, and purpose. Why did the society we were powering up seem hellbent on stunting its population's emotional growth, stability, and well-being? Couldn't we ask better, more elevated questions, triggering greater ingenuity? Rather than asking "What's in it for me?" Why not ask, "What do I get to create today, how can I best serve, who needs more of what I have to offer?" Thinking differently saw me producing different results, it was fascinating thought-work. I was visualising, seeing, speaking, and talking things into existence. Over time and 'dream work' compound interest, these things began manifesting in my life. My mind was becoming an optimal manifesting machine, and life was starting to take on magical new imprints.

I won a holiday to Italy, got a lovely part-time job teaching Dutch to the corporate agency of European Medicines. From there, I booked a sweet little gig in a theatrical piece at the Finborough, where casting director Leo Davis was in attendance one night, which led to being cast in Stephen Frears' TV show *Quiz*. Life was moving swimmingly, and as it did, my business mentor kept urging me on to package this content and sell what I knew.

At first, I thought he meant just taking up a tiny corner in a library and talking about the merits of your invisible powers. But pretty soon, he was suggesting I develop my own website, get marketing, create a program, because honestly, the systems I was sharing, shook *him* with excitement, "People need to know about this, Gracy, the world needs to know about these things," he kept saying.

The dream engineer in me was beginning to emerge.

We are made up of molecules and electrolytes, and at our core, and at every microscopic level in the centre of our cells, lies a void. At the centre of this void, often depicted in fairy tales and mythology as the cavernous mine work of the heart, beats our own creativity. Its infinite wisdom is powerful enough to send tremors penetrating so deep into the human psyche that we mere mortals, conditioned to fear the greatness of our human potential, run rings around it to avoid the necessary inner confrontation needed to unleash its brilliance onto the world.

If creativity sits in the void and its projections hurled outwardly, it must be our electrolytes, the light wave particles, that agitate and thrust these formations into forward-moving motion. Intensifying our focus outward, steering our consciousness into the concentrated collective field, and mingling with the collective cohort to produce any number of determined or undetermined outcomes. Our manifestations become a chain of light, focused energy, flowing into the forms we wish to mould into being. (Or not, as the case may be.) We are vibratory beings, bringing vibrational forms into existence. The less conscious we are, or connected we are to our main source, the greater the scope for trial and inevitable error.

There is both a science and a philosophy behind manifesting our dream desires. When striving for success, we must first tap into this inner game. Life is a beautiful, powerful, and compelling mirror of illusions, and we are the originals from which all else is reflected. Stepping into the arena without awareness can create as much devastation as it can goodness, on a dime.

Expansion in any positive direction is about wealth creation, and wealth creation comes in many different shapes and forms. Generating wealth in relationships and wealth in business, wealth in health and wealth in love, generating wealth in every single kind of relationship you can imagine, be that with your plants, your money, the self-talk swirling around your mind, is all about your power of focus. By your self-directed focus and attention to them, you expand and appreciate these relationships more. 'Looking', what I lovingly refer to as the observer effect, has the seeds of expansion within it. Just simply *looking* at the desired object in question has the ability to reveal the true nature of your relationship with it and what is most required to affect growth and real transformation.

When we align this fundamental way of thinking, everything we touch in the outer realm becomes a direct reflection of our innermost realities. Flow with the non-resistant thought-forms of your deepest desires, to allow them to play their part on the stage of creation with expansion.

Breaking Free: Why Dreamers Must Own Their Path

We are living in times of rapid instability and chaos. Most will agree that having the luxury to dream is a privilege few can afford, and yet to choose *not* to utilise the unique gifts we were born with comes at an even greater cost to Self and humanity. As life gets bleaker and bleaker, to carve a way out of the deep, dark trenches is to dream a vision for a new earth, a new way of being and co-existing in the world, and to hold that vision as a constant, is bravery. To see a thing as you would have it in your mind's eye, regardless of all kinds of commotion to the contrary on the outside. We are a collective consciousness possessing equal amounts of the same dreamlike substance, expressed uniquely, through an individual soul prism. Building a business that helps the individual wake up to their own unique talents and raison d'être ensures a brighter, happier vibrational planet, for the younger generators we leave in our wake to grow and evolve from. To embed this new vision and outlook for the world, a paradigm shift is required. (Perhaps the Donald Trumps of this lifetime are making it easier for us to double down and focus these shifts faster.)

My offerings are for all the dreamers, risers, and creators of this world, for those brave enough to walk the path less travelled. Holding onto your dreams as currency, and finding ways of maintaining them and keeping them alive, is hard for anyone. It is therefore, perhaps harder still for those who feel disenfranchised. For women—especially women of colour, those with disabilities, and anyone living on the fringes of society—learning to value their dreams as currency and stream them into the world with firm financial backing has the power to create a powerful odyssey of change.

The Momentum Formula - Turning Passion Into Cash Flow

I had resisted marketing for *so* long!

An essential part of the business that I hated doing the most. To go from being an actress with an agent to having to market my wares myself is not something I *preferred*. And definitely not in my wheelhouse of genius, it is a skill I had to acquire.

I had knowledge, a service, and a product I 1000% believed in, but packaging it up and selling it in a way that folk would want to buy? Ugh.

It wasn't until I was really able to recognise and identify the people in my tribe I wanted to serve, and who were calling out for what I had to offer, that I began to feel a passion stirring to communicate my message effectively. To dream as big and as bodaciously as I had come into this world, and to act as a visible example both in my own creative life and in my business.

I was starting to wake up to how damn important it was to facilitate an offering and a place where people could thrive. Where imaginations could accelerate, talents could come together for the specific remit of expanding their own unique gifts to collectively raise the consciousness of the planet. Thriving is contagious, and just like I expressed earlier, when our molecules start to dance with delight, not just humanity, but this entire, living, breathing universe catches fire, and like a flaming planet, we raise the vibrations.

The more conscious we become, the more we can determine how we want to seed, plant and grow our creative investments. Women, though not strictly isolated to this one group, are well-versed in raising an army so that communities and wider circles beyond themselves can thrive. We know instinctively how to make things happen *inclusively* so that everyone benefits and winners are created all round.

Dreaming big, and seeing the vision blueprint of what I wanted to create expanding twenty years into the future, gave me the strength and motivation needed to be cheeky as f**k, not give two hoots what others thought, and to continue to live my life, my vision, and my dreams out large. Being in your creative dojo is key to "getting on" your cash flow mojo, and lighting up with clarity and confidence the vision for a new economy, one based in harmony and equality.

Scaling Your Dream (Building a Business That Aligns With You)

I was beginning to develop a really healthy relationship with my business, not just 'winging and praying' it, but I was starting to intricately understand the nature of Suits & Saints as an extension of myself. How it functioned and what it needed in order to support my dreams and goals of walking my talk, following my bliss, and teaching others how to do the same.

The clearer I had my business systems in place, the better I could make decisions about what best, next step strategies I needed to make, what kind of team I wanted to build to support the ethos of my company, and the members of my tribe it was attracting to it. I learned the most exciting part of all about business: Scaling your business is essentially code to the Artist or Creative for *scaling your dreams*.

The bigger and more fearless I could dream, the more time I could put aside for planning and strategy. I was laying the groundwork to spot opportunities as they arose, to think outside of the box, and to lay down a vision so clearly that the roadmap to leveraging my wealthy dreams became inevitable. I wanted to become so excited about life that bouncing out of bed every morning became a visceral act of gratitude. To find passion and pass it on, to think of more ways of creating huge, audacious transformation in self and others through the power of creativity; how much better could it get than this?

"When you get clear on your vision, everything changes. Current problems become small, creativity gets pumping and conversations get interesting, but none of that can happen without clarity." ~ Dan Martell

Future-proof your dreams by 10X-ing them, getting clear and getting creative. Dream Big. So that you become a magnet to the scale and force of the Universe's power and flow. Once you have this down, create strategies for a clear pathway to success.

Exercise:

Armchair Flying Your 10 X Vision

Step 1: Sit in a comfy seat or on a meditation pillow, close your eyes, and take a few deep breaths in and out to settle your nervous system. Begin the journey of allowing yourself to go within and dream BIG. Let the landscape of your mind become a fearless state of limitless possibilities. Go wild! Allow everything that has ever set your soul on fire to flash before you. What would life look like if nothing stood in the way of this boundless imagination? Now slap on a dash of 'the crazy'. Explore the avenues that might ignite your passion if you could dive headfirst into the adventure. Who would you be with? What would you be doing, what problems would you be solving? Make your mission so huge that you cannot be distracted by the small stuff. What insane ideas are you manufacturing? Artists, creatives, and entrepreneurs are problem solvers and our imaginations to go to work by filling in the void? What void are you filling?

Step 2: Now we call for some clarity. We have zoomed out wide into a whole technicolor spectrum of mayhem (and hopefully madness), it's time now to zoom *in* and latch onto the things that really caused our boats to float. Let's do this by scripting out our current time reality. What does a typical day in your life look like for you? What routines and habits do you have? Do you get up to go to work? If so, what time? Who do you meet? Who are your work colleagues, family members, and friends? Get real specific. The more detail, the better. Now, allow yourself to span as far out as ten years into the future. Answer the very same questions (and more) with the same amount of detail in the first person. You reach out to meet your future Self, who are you with? What are you working on? What kind of team do you have to support your grand adventures and wild ideas? Where do you hang out socially? Which family members are with you on the journey? Be as detailed as you can, as if that future day were here right now.

When you know with crystal clear precision what you are working on, you become unstoppable. As long as you dare to dream big, the scope of achieving greatness is unending. You become so motivated that the obstacles that come your way (and there will be many) will not deter you from success.

Enjoy unleashing your wild spirit and discovering the details that matter to you most.

From here on in, with this blueprint in front of you, you have created the means to populate your calendar with new daily activities. With your North Star acting as a shining beacon of light to guide the way. Every day becomes a joy to bounce out of bed and give thanks for. Trust me, when you have an *almost* impossible mission and you fill your mind with as many creative ways to make it happen, you'll have a head full of entertainment and innovation so spectacular, Netflix, Sky, and Paramount combined couldn't hold a candle to your creations!

"If you don't know where you're going,
you'll end up some place else!" —Yogi Berra.

Wealth, Impact, and The Future of Lightworker Entrepreneurs

When dreams grow, cash flows. I have to imagine that to artists, this is music to our ears; we think everything in reverse, which is actually the nature of an entrepreneur. Like the entrepreneur, we live to create, build, and magic things out of that rare air we strive to be in. We live for the art, not for the dough. At least, from my tiny perspective, this is how I imagine most other artists think.

But we have to survive too.

And when we recognise that bringing our creation to life is *vital* – not indulgent – it shifts everything.

Marketing, messaging, and networking become sacred acts – offerings in honour of humanity.

Suppressing your vision doesn't serve the world – it starves it.

Now you carry a new awareness: that partnering with your business as a conscious, caring entity isn't just for you - it's for all of us.

"You do your dream flow, I'll do the cash flow!" ~ said the Business to the Entrepreneur.

By aligning my creative drive with business acumen, I found myself in my happy place—where the work, albeit challenging, becomes deeply satisfying and rewarding.

These coordinates we find ourselves in, in the jungles of time and space, where Earth's inhabitants appear to be on the precipice of birthing new dimensions into being, are delicate, vulnerable times, and so much hangs in the balance. There is ample scope to falter, and yet so much magic is available to us here. Systems as we know them may well be in the process of collapsing, and this is understandably a terrifying prospect. But let's not forget the void where true creativity arises, and the currents that carry us toward these vortices, draw us closer to our treasures. To re-imagine our humanity, beyond race, gender, rich or poor class systems is to re-imagine a world where all get to live, support, and thrive under a different set of values and co-creating. Where many of the old norms are obsolete and individual talents, gifts, and services create a chain of positive effects so powerful that jealousy, inequality and the like, no longer act as seductive bargaining chips that we bring to an exclusive table.

Lillian Jaques

Founder of Harmonix LLC

https://www.linkedin.com/company/harmonix-llc
https://www.facebook.com/profile.php?id=61554300496755#
https://harmonix.click/
https://open.spotify.com/artist/4jiEIBWJfz7bOp6Chhz6TG

Lilly Jaques is the founder of Harmonix LLC, an innovative A.I. think tank dedicated to empowering artists in the rapidly evolving landscape of artificial intelligence. With a mission to demystify the "scary" world of A.I., Lilly and Harmonix LLC help artists integrate cutting-edge A.I. solutions into their creative processes, offering tools and strategies they might not have previously considered. As a young entrepreneur, Lilly is passionate about globally influencing youth to reach their fullest potential, fostering a new generation of creators who harness the power of technology for artistic growth and expression.

The Quantum Dreams of Harmonix LLC

By Lillian Jaques

Some mornings, I wake up and the world feels... off. Like stepping out of sync with reality, finding myself in a slightly altered dimension. It's a feeling reminiscent of *The Matrix* – a sense that the reality I'm operating in, particularly at the helm of Harmonix LLC, is constantly shifting, accelerating into a future that feels both exhilarating and profoundly unreal. The pace of technological change, the sheer potential held within algorithms and processing power, can be disorienting. It demands a constant recalibration of what's possible. Like the White Queen in Lewis Carroll's *Through the Looking-Glass*, I, too, sometimes believe as many as six impossible things before breakfast. And one of those impossible things, the one that fuels Harmonix LLC, is the betterment of humanity – a potential that has never felt more achievable than it does right now.

This isn't just gradual progress anymore. We're seeing a convergence of powerful forces: Artificial Intelligence (AI) is rapidly evolving, the potential of Artificial General Intelligence (AGI) looms on the horizon, and the dawn of Quantum Computing promises fundamentally new ways to solve problems. **With these new technologies taking hold, truly aggressive expansion towards goals once considered pure science fiction is no longer a pipe dream; it's rapidly becoming a practical reality. Given this acceleration, the question becomes unavoidable: Why *not* a cure for type 1 diabetes?** If we have tools capable of reshaping industries and cracking previously unsolvable codes, shouldn't we aim them squarely at the conditions that cause so much human suffering?

Steve Jobs famously spoke about connecting the dots, looking backward. He said, "You can't connect the dots looking forward; you can only connect them looking backwards. So, you have to trust that the dots will somehow connect in your future." Starting Harmonix LLC often felt like placing a dot in the dark, a significant departure from the path I once envisioned within the Senate walls. Looking back now, the trauma and disillusionment of that experience were the painful, necessary catalysts. Harmonix LLC, with its focus on artificial intelligence and the horizon of quantum computing, is the next dot. Trusting it will connect? That's the daily act of faith entrepreneurship requires.

It's a leap into the unknown, guided by the wisdom of another icon – this one a Canadian legend from right here in Ontario, Wayne Gretzky. He famously said, "You miss 100% of the shots you don't take." Founding Harmonix LLC, especially with its ambitious aims, is taking the shot. It's refusing to be paralyzed by the past or the uncertainty of the future. It's about aiming for something potentially transformative, even if the target seems impossibly distant right now.

And the target for Harmonix LLC, the ultimate "shot," involves harnessing the very technology that makes the world feel like *The Matrix*: advanced computing. We explore AI now, developing algorithms and testing potential applications, always looking toward the quantum horizon. The dream? To leverage these powerful tools for breakthroughs that truly matter, particularly in areas like drug development and complex disease modeling. Seeing developments like the one MIT researchers announced back in late 2023 – using AI to identify a whole new class of antibiotic candidates capable of killing resilient bacteria like MRSA – fuels that ambition. It's tangible proof that AI can "see" patterns and possibilities hidden from human researchers, offering shortcuts through previously intractable problems.

That possibility sparks immense hope. But I'll be honest: I'm scared. Deeply scared. Because my most fervent hope, the driving force behind so much of this, is deeply personal. Can a computer, even a quantum one, find a cure for type 1 diabetes? Decades of medical research, countless expert opinions, and my own lived experience scream the same word: "incurable." It's hard to hold onto hope when the weight of that label feels so absolute. How can silicon and code possibly succeed where generations of brilliant human minds have stalled?

When I write that my life very much feels like *The Matrix*, it's because, in many ways, it does – particularly in the sense of the living hell that being insulin-dependent in this day and age can be. Navigating the daily complexities, the constant vigilance, the societal misunderstandings – it often feels like battling invisible forces within a system not designed for you.

Yet, a part of me, maybe like a piece of toast popping unexpectedly from the toaster as my brother Ted might say, refuses to let go. A stubborn voice insists, *You have to be stupid enough to believe it's possible.* Perhaps that's the core of it – the necessary suspension of disbelief, the irrational optimism required to chase moonshots.

But it absolutely cannot be blind optimism. The realist in me knows the pitfalls, and they run deeper than just technological hurdles. We must grapple directly and honestly with the pervasive issue of **AI bias, often referred to as machine learning bias or algorithm bias.** It's crucial to understand what this means: **it refers specifically to AI systems that produce biased results, results that unfortunately reflect and actively perpetuate existing human biases within our society. This includes entrenching historical inequalities and cementing current social disparities.** It's not just some abstract technical glitch; **bias can embed itself insidiously within the initial training data we feed the machines, within the very structure of the algorithm, or manifest clearly in the predictions and outputs the algorithm ultimately produces.**

When this bias goes unaddressed, the consequences are severe and far-reaching. It actively **hinders people's ability to participate fully and equally in the economy and in society at large.** Far from unlocking potential, unchecked bias actually **reduces AI's overall**

potential for good, limiting its applicability and effectiveness. For instance, **businesses cannot truly benefit from systems that consistently produce distorted results.** More importantly, biased systems **foster deep mistrust among already marginalized communities, including people of color, women, people with disabilities – a group whose challenges I know firsthand – the LGBTQ community, and countless other groups** who have historically faced discrimination.

This brings the danger into sharp focus when we consider the pursuit of a cure for type 1 diabetes. If these powerful AI models learn primarily from existing medical literature – a literature base saturated with the word "incurable" regarding T1D – what happens? The danger is precisely that the AI might inherit this conclusion not as a challenge to be overcome, but as a fundamental truth, a boundary condition programmed into its very core. It might learn the "fact" that T1D is incurable so thoroughly that it dismisses data points or novel hypotheses pointing towards a cure simply because they contradict the overwhelming consensus in its training data. We risk creating algorithmic blind spots, reinforcing the very limitations we hope to transcend. The machine could become incredibly efficient at managing diabetes within the current paradigm, but be fundamentally incapable of *imagining* its eradication because it has, in essence, absorbed the historical pessimism of the field. It's a potential future where the machine, lacking human intuition or defiance, simply types the word "incurable" back at us, echoing the limitations we fed it. Addressing AI bias, therefore, isn't just an ethical necessity; it's fundamental to ensuring these powerful tools don't inadvertently slam the door on the very breakthroughs we desperately need.

This dual challenge – chasing a moonshot cure while simultaneously fighting the ingrained biases that could prevent us from ever reaching it – is monumental. It requires vigilance, conscious effort, and a willingness to question everything, including the data we rely on. But facing this challenge head-on? **Honestly? I have no problems dying on this hill.**

For me, personally and professionally, it feels like the hill I've been waiting for my whole life. It's where my lived experience, my technological ambitions, and my fight for equity converge.

And if I've learned anything in this lifetime, if the struggles and setbacks have taught me one crucial lesson, it's this: You only get one shot, one opportunity, to seize everything you ever wanted, in one moment. This venture, Harmonix LLC, feels like that moment, that opportunity. **And I *will* capture it.** I owe it to myself, and I owe it to everyone else waiting for technology to live up to its promise.

So, that's the tightrope Harmonix LLC walks. We dream of quantum leaps and cures, fueled by accelerating technology and Gretzky's call to action. We trust, like Jobs suggested, that the dots will eventually connect. But we do so with eyes wide open to the risks, the fears, and the absolute necessity of building these tools responsibly, actively combating bias in all its forms. The dream isn't just about finding *a* cure; it's about building a future where technology serves humanity's highest aspirations, overcoming not just diseases, but also the limitations of our past beliefs, ensuring *everyone* benefits from the impossible things we dare to achieve before breakfast.

Dr. Gina Kuhn-Robatin

Founder and CEO of Dr. Gina's Transformation Academy
Entrepreneur, Speaker

https://www.linkedin.com/in/dr-gina-kuhn-robatin-9814402a7/
https://www.facebook.com/gina.kuhnrobatin

Dr. Gina Kuhn-Robatin is an award-winning entrepreneur, professional singer, medical massage therapist, and expert speaker. As the founder of both Dr. Gina's Transformation Academy, LLC and D.R.E.A.M. In Motion. She empowers women to live their dreams, balance career and family, live authentically and with purpose. Beyond her professional success, her greatest achievement is being a devoted mother of two sons. Together, they traveled the country through their family singing ministry, Gina has sung and spoke in 49 States, touching lives while leading by example-demonstrating resilience, sacrifice, and unwavering love. She has instilled Leadership and compassion in her sons, showing them the power of perseverance and faith. Through challenges and triumphs, Dr. Gina Kuhn-Robatin remains a beacon of strength, proving that motherhood and success can coexist. Her story is a testament to the heart of a mother- one who gives endlessly, loves fiercely, and rises stronger.

From Business to Stage: Embracing the Unexpected Path of Reinvention

By Dr. Gina Kuhn-Robatin

Success in business and in life rarely follows a straight path. It twists, it turns, and sometimes, it demands that we make bold, life-altering moves. My journey as an entrepreneur has been defined by resilience, reinvention, and the courage to embrace the unknown. The few moments faced a life-changing health crisis that forced me to pivot in ways I never imagined.

The Unexpected Challenge

Entrepreneurship has been my life for decades. I had built businesses, navigated industries, and thrived in the dynamic world of commerce. But no amount of business knowledge could have prepared me for the moment when my body betrayed me. A stroke stopped me in my tracks, forcing me into a nine-month battle to regain my strength, my independence, and ultimately, my future.

Everything changed in an instant. The go-getter, the entrepreneur, the woman who had spent her life building and growing businesses was suddenly unable to do the simplest of tasks. Those months were a test of endurance, not just physically, but mentally and emotionally as well. Every day was a fight to regain what I had lost, but I refused to accept defeat.

A Hard Decision

As difficult as my recovery was, an even harder reality hit me: my business could not wait for me. The world of entrepreneurship doesn't pause, and while I had built something successful, I had to face the trust, and I had to let it go. After months of fighting to stand on my own two feet again, I had to make one of the most painful decisions of my life: I had to sell my business.

Letting go wasn't just about losing a business. It was about saying goodbye to something I had poured my heart and soul into. It was about releasing control, admitting that my life had changed, and accepting that the path forward looked different than I had planned. If there's one thing I have learned through years of entrepreneurship, it's that when one door closes, another one opens. You just have to be bold enough to walk through it.

The Pivot: A Leaf of Faith

With my business gone, still healing time needed, and no clear path forward, I faced a crossroads. I could dwell on what I had lost, or I could seize the opportunity to create something new. My family and I chose the latter.

We didn't just pivot—we leaped!

We sold our home, packed up our lives, and left behind the familiar for a brand new chapter. Our destination? Nashville, Tennessee. Our mission? To take our professional singing career to a whole new level.

Singing had always been a part of our lives, but now, it became our purpose, our passion, and our business. The decision wasn't made lightly. It required sacrifice, selling not just our house but having to leave our friends and family as well. It meant stepping into the unknown with nothing but faith and determination to guide us.

And then the miracle happened!

From Loss to Opportunity: Signing with a Record Label

Before making the bold move to Tennessee, doors began to open. We caught the attention of a record label that believed in us and our music.

What started as a leap of faith suddenly sent us on a full-fledged touring career. Before we knew it, we were on the road, traveling full-time in our touring bus, bringing our music and message of hope to audiences across the nation.

The transition from entrepreneur to full-time performer was exhilarating and terrifying all at the same time. While I was no stranger to business, this was an entirely new arena. Touring had proven many new challenges. Not many people realize how much of yourself you must give. I've always said, "Leave it all on the stage." What I meant by that is, give your audiences, first, your authentic self and give it all you got! If you're not spent when you come off that stage, you haven't fully done your job. Touring wasn't just about performing, it was about branding, marketing, and building our mission of hope through our music.

The same skill that had once helped me grow my previous businesses became the foundation for our success in the music industry.

Sales and Marketing

Just like in any business, we had to market our music, book performances, and learn how to best engage with our audiences. Every opportunity was a new moment to connect with people and bring them new hope and encouragement.

Adaptability: Touring meant constant change and sacrifice. New cities, new venues, and new challenges. Being adaptable has always been a strength of mine. I embraced the fast-paced nature of the industry.

Resilience: A music career, like business careers, is unpredictable. Some nights, the crowds were massive. Other nights, they were intimate. We always looked at every opportunity as a chance to make a profound impact on others' lives.

A Life on the Road

Life on a tour bus was a world away from the structured routine of my previous businesses. It was non-stop travel, early mornings, sometimes late nights, and endless energy poured into every moment. We weren't just running a business, we were living our brand and our mission.

For all its challenges, there was nothing quite like road life. Every mile travelled, every stage taken, every personal connection reminded me why we had made this bold move.

We weren't just chasing our dreams and our purpose, we were building a legacy of love through music, personal engagement, and encouragement into others' lives.

The sacrifices we had made were worth it. We had traded comfort for purpose, security for passion, and predictability for adventure. In doing so, we had created a life that was richer and more fulfilling than we could have ever imagined.

The Power of Reinvention

Looking back, I realize that my boldest business moves weren't just about strategies or decisions, they were about the willingness to reinvent myself after my stroke.

Losing my business could have been the end of my entrepreneurial story, but instead, it became the beginning of something even greater. I learned that success isn't about clinging to what was, it's about embracing what can be.

This experience reinforced one of the greatest truths of my journey:

Entrepreneurs aren't defined by their businesses. They're defined by their ability to adapt, evolve, and create new opportunities, no matter the obstacles.

Where I Stand Today

After years on the road, traveling coast to coast and impacting lives through our music, I carry with me a profound sense of gratitude. I have walked through loss, embraced change, and emerged stronger than ever. My path has never been conventional, but it has always been bold.

Today, as I continue to build, create, and empower others, I do so with the knowledge that no challenge is too great and no pivot is too daunting. Whether business, music, or life itself, the key to success is the courage to get back up and keep moving forward.

And that's exactly what I intend to do!

Nana Adjoa Sifa Amponsah

Founder of Guzakuza

https://www.linkedin.com/in/nana-adjoa-sifa-amponsah-91099950/
http://www.nadjoasifa.org/
https://guzakuza.com/

Nana Adjoa A. Sifa is a gender- lens entrepreneur and ecosystem builder committed to driving change in social investment, agrifood system and amplifying women's voices. As Founder of Guzakuza, she has ignited over 9,000 women across 36 countries, equipping them to build scalable, sustainable businesses through initiatives like Ignite Africa, MentorHer, WiFAI, and SheFarms. A World Economic Forum Global Shaper, UN Women UK Delegate, and NYU-GWSLP Fellow, Nana has shaped global conversations on women, entrepreneurship, and climate. She has spoken on high-level panels, including presenting the Berlin Charter at the G20.Recognised with awards like the UK's Inspiring Women Award and Africa 40 Under 40, her work has been featured in The New York Times, Spore Magazine, and DW TV. She also founded The FeMail, a platform championing women's voices in business. Nana is passionate about unlocking capital, reshaping systems, and creating opportunities for women to thrive in agrifood and beyond.

Unapologetically Visible: The Bold Business Move That Changed Everything

By Nana Adjoa Sifa Amponsah

There was a time I preferred to stay behind the scenes—building, nurturing, and dreaming. I poured myself into projects that gave women tools to thrive, launched programs that changed lives, and led movements that sparked transformation across Africa. But for a while, I did it quietly. I believed the work would speak for itself.

Until I realized: Movements don't just need momentum—they need a face, a voice, a light.

That light had to be mine.

Becoming unapologetically visible wasn't vanity. It was strategy. It was survival. It was the boldest business move I ever made. And it changed everything.

This is the story of how stepping into the spotlight didn't just amplify my brand—it ignited a continent-wide mission, opened global doors, and gave thousands of women permission to shine, too.

The Quiet Fire

I used to hide my ambition like it was a secret. It was as if I thought being quiet would make me more humble, more palatable. **But quietly building something powerful in the shadows doesn't make you less of a force—it just keeps you invisible.**

For years, I kept my passion locked away, convinced that the work would speak for itself. I poured my energy into Guzakuza, SheFarms, and Ignite, touching lives across Africa, helping women find their strength in agribusiness. But as I watched these incredible women grow, something inside me whispered, *You're doing amazing work, but no one knows it's you behind the wheel.*

At the core, I wasn't just hiding my voice—I was hiding **myself**. And while my programs and initiatives were creating change, the world needed to see the woman driving it all. It was time to stop dimming my light, to stop pretending that staying small would make me more effective.

There was a time when I preferred to stay in the background. I thought the work would speak for itself. I was building something incredible. Women across Africa were changing the agribusiness landscape. They were creating jobs, feeding families, and empowering entire communities. But I was quietly behind the scenes—building, nurturing, dreaming. It felt safer to stay there, especially as a woman in a male-dominated industry.

I remember the early days of Guzakuza—back when we were just starting to turn the wheels of impact. I didn't want attention. I wanted the programs I created to shine, not my face. I launched SheFarms and Ignite to support women in agriculture, and I poured my heart into it. But no matter how much I pushed, how many lives I impacted, I often felt invisible. No one really knew who was behind these efforts. I realized that despite the ripple effect of our work, something was missing. **My own voice.**

I'll never forget the first time I was asked to speak at a large international event—alongside some of the biggest names in agribusiness and development. I was terrified. My stomach twisted. Here I was, in the same room with giants, and I was just a "quiet leader" from Ghana. At that moment, it hit me: I was so focused on the impact of my work that I had forgotten to **show up** for it. If I wanted to make a bigger difference, I needed to stand up, be seen, and unapologetically share the story of why I was doing this work.

Key Lesson: *Sometimes, we spend so much time proving our worth with results that we forget to amplify our voices. Visibility isn't vanity—it's the signal that your work matters.*

I know many women reading this can relate.

We do the work.

We hold the vision.

We push quietly from the background, thinking humility means hiding.

For years, I led programs that impacted thousands. I created fellowships, built a team, and raised future leaders. I had a full heart, but my brand? My voice? It was whispering in the background of my own success story. I showed up in rooms, but not fully. I was visible... but not seen.

And it worked—until it didn't.

The fire was there. The mission was clear. But something was missing. My movement needed momentum, and for that, it needed a face. It needed a story. It needed me to stop hiding.

The Turning Point

The decision to become *unapologetically visible* wasn't one grand, dramatic moment—it was a series of small, deliberate choices that built up over time. I had to rewrite the script I'd been living by. The one that said, *"Let your work speak for you."* But here's what I learned the hard way: in business, silence isn't humility—it's a missed opportunity. Invisibility can cost you partnerships, funding, recognition, and even your voice.

My bold business move? I stopped waiting for permission to be seen. I gave it to myself.

I remember sitting at a conference where one of the speakers said, *"You can't be a secret and a success at the same time."* It hit me like lightning. I had built programs that had impacted thousands of women across Africa and beyond. I had supported founders who were scaling sustainable agribusinesses, raising capital, and changing their communities. Yet, I was still hesitant to fully step into my story. Still deflecting praise. Still pushing others forward while quietly standing in the background.

One day, a friend looked me in the eye and said, *"Nana, you've been coaching women to show up, but you're still hiding your own brilliance. Why are you afraid of your light?"* I didn't have a good answer. I only knew I was tired of shrinking to fit the room.

I remember the moment everything finally shifted. I was invited to a high-level event. One of those global gatherings where decisions are made, partnerships are formed, and change is shaped. As I sat in that room, surrounded by leaders, I realized something: I belonged there. My work belonged in that room. But my name wasn't known. My face wasn't recognized. People knew the programs I led—but not the woman behind them.

That day, I made a decision that scared me:

I would stop shrinking.
I would stop apologizing.
I would become unapologetically visible.

Not for ego. Not for applause. But because the mission demanded it. Because the women I serve needed to see a bold example of what's possible. Because too many powerful women were hiding in the shadows, waiting for permission to shine. And maybe—just maybe—if I went first, they would too.

So I started saying **yes** to visibility—not just passively allowing it, but intentionally pursuing it.

I began sharing the behind-the-scenes of my journey: the wins, the struggles, the failures, the pivots. I spoke openly about the time I nearly gave up on Guzakuza because I was burnt out and funding was running low. I talked about navigating motherhood while running an organization across multiple time zones. I shared about the imposter syndrome I felt walking into global rooms and how I coached myself through it.

I stopped downplaying my achievements. When I was featured in *The New York Times*, I shared it. When I won the UK Inspiring Women Award, I celebrated it publicly. Not out of ego, but out of intention. Because I realized that **every time a Black African woman is visible for the right reasons, we chip away at the narrative that says we don't exist in certain rooms.**

I rebuilt my online presence. I reintroduced myself—on LinkedIn, on my website, even on WhatsApp. I realized that people support what they can see. And if no one can find you, they can't fund you, collaborate with you, or learn from you.

That shift—**from quietly impactful to boldly visible**—was the turning point. Doors I didn't even know existed began to open. Global platforms invited me to speak. Institutions reached out for partnerships. Women who saw themselves in my story started emailing me saying, *"Because of your post, I finally applied for that grant."*

Visibility wasn't vanity. It was strategy.

Visibility Is a Growth Strategy

For a long time, I thought visibility was something you earned *after* you'd succeeded. Now I know: **visibility is how you grow**. It's not a reward—it's a requirement.

When I shifted my mindset from "stay low and build" to "build loudly and intentionally," things started to align. Opportunities didn't just knock—they found me. My inbox changed. The level of conversations I was having changed. Investors, collaborators, media houses—they started showing up not because I was doing different work, but because I was **showing up differently.**

I began to see that the women I was mentoring were facing the same hurdle. Brilliant ideas. Powerful impact. But invisible. I'd ask, *"Where can I find you online?"* They'd shy away. Websites outdated, bios half-written, LinkedIn deserted. Not because they weren't proud of their work—but because they hadn't been taught that **how you show up matters as much as what you do.**

So I started weaving visibility into everything I taught. I encouraged my fellows to pitch themselves for speaking engagements, update their digital homes, share their behind-the-scenes, and own their expertise. Not in a performative way—but in an authentic, human way that builds trust.

And guess what? They began to grow too. Visibility creates momentum.

It creates **believability**, too. People can only invest in what they understand. And they can only understand what they can see and feel. Your story. Your values. Your voice. That's what makes people lean in.

Even corporations and institutions, especially those who want to fund or partner with women-led ventures, are scanning the room for those who are already visible. It's not about being perfect—it's about being present.

The Bold Move to Be Unapologetically Visible

Stepping into visibility was not a magical transformation. It didn't come with flashing lights or viral videos. It started with a trembling voice, a shaking hand, and the quiet courage to say, "Here I am."

I didn't wake up one day and feel confident. I decided to show up, even when I didn't. I remember the first time I said "yes" to a major speaking engagement that made my knees wobble. I had been invited to speak at a global event—alongside people whose names echoed in boardrooms and newsrooms. And there I was, thinking: *Will my story matter? Will they take me seriously?*

But I showed up. I spoke anyway. And something incredible happened: people listened. Not just to the facts, but to the fire in my belly. They connected. They reached out. Doors opened. That's when I realized: Our stories are bridges—our presence is power.

And so, I kept showing up.

I said yes to panels, podcasts, features, and interviews. I stopped hiding behind my logo and started standing beside it. I updated my bios. I told my story—not just the highlights, but the heartbreaks, the rebuilding, the why behind the what.

I started sharing photos that scared me. I claimed titles I used to whisper—Founder, CEO, Changemaker. I allowed myself to be seen in full color, not just in bullet points.

Was it uncomfortable? Absolutely.

But with every step, I felt myself expanding into the woman I was always becoming.

What changed? Everything.

People no longer just wanted to support my work—they wanted to support me. Brands started inviting me to the table. Women started writing, "Because of your story, I didn't give up." Investors began to say yes, because now, they knew who stood behind the numbers.

What Changed

Looking back, it's wild to think how many of us are conditioned to believe that staying small is the same as being humble. That silence is strength. But I learned that when you are building something world-changing, the world needs to see you.

I didn't just gain followers or features. I gained influence. My voice now echoes in rooms I used to dream about. And with every opportunity, I carry thousands of women with me—women who never saw someone like them in spaces like that. Until now.

That's the thing about being unapologetically visible: ***It's not about being the loudest. It's about being authentic. The most you.***

Because when you are visible in your truth, your people find you. Your partners find you. Your purpose multiplies.

A New Kind of Leadership

Being unapologetically visible didn't just change how the world saw me—it transformed how I saw myself as a leader. I went from feeling like an imposter to realizing that I had earned every space I entered. I stopped questioning my worth and began owning the fact that my work, my story, and my voice were just as valuable as anyone else's in the room.

Visibility allowed me to step into a new leadership role—not just as a founder, but as someone who could inspire, empower, and raise up others to do the same.

In the past, I thought leadership was about having all the answers. But now, I see it's about creating space for others to find their voice. It's about being a beacon of possibility, not perfection.

I've watched countless women in my network—many of them fellow entrepreneurs—struggle with the idea of being seen. Many of them, just like I did, stayed small, waited to be "discovered," or felt like their ideas weren't ready for the spotlight. But as I stepped forward, I saw the shift. When they saw me being unapologetically visible, they started showing up, too.

They started leading with their stories, their strengths, and their unfiltered truths. They understood that visibility wasn't about popularity; it was about purpose.

The Ripple Effect

The most incredible part of becoming visible wasn't the accolades or the recognition—it was the ripple effect that followed. The women who reached out to say they'd started their businesses because of something I shared. The founders who finally stopped dimming themselves, who said, "If Nana can do it, so can I."

That's the magic of being unapologetically visible: It's not just your success you amplify—it's the success of everyone who sees themselves in you.

When I took that leap, I didn't just shift my business trajectory. I shifted the way women in my community showed up for themselves. And those women—thousands of them—are now leading movements of their own. From rural farms to tech startups, I'm seeing women stand up, speak out, and take up space in ways that were once unimaginable.

And all of this was possible because I decided to show up. Because I chose to be unapologetically visible.

Call to Action

So, here's the challenge I leave you with: What's keeping you hidden? What parts of your story, your business, or your gifts are you holding back from the world?

Visibility isn't about being perfect. It's about being authentic. It's about showing up in your full, unapologetic power, knowing that your presence has the potential to change lives—yours and others.

We, as women entrepreneurs, have far too much power to stay small. It's time to stop shrinking.

Stand up. Speak up. Be unapologetically visible.

Your movement is waiting. Your people are waiting. And the world?

The world needs to see what you're capable of.

When I stopped hiding, everything changed—not just for me, but for every woman who needed to see someone like her leading from the front.

Krizel Rodriguez

Founder of Leading Lady Network

https://www.linkedin.com/in/krizelrodriguez
https://facebook.com/leadingladynetwork
https://www.instagram.com/leading_lady_network
https://leadingladynetwork.com
https://krizelrodriguez.com

Krizel Rodriguez, known as "La Reina of Leadership," has redefined resilience and empowerment. Once convinced that weight loss surgery was her only path to being seen, she faced a life-altering challenge when a one-in-a-million infectious disease left her bed-ridden and fighting for life. Determined to transform adversity into triumph, she vowed to chase every dream if she survived. Today, as an entrepreneur, TEDx speaker, devoted mother, and Mrs. Texas Plus USA 2025, Krizel leads with unstoppable passion. As founder and CEO of the Leading Lady Network, she has created a vibrant community where women of all shapes, sizes, and shades rediscover their worth. Her groundbreaking TAILOR Method personalizes leadership strategies, while the exclusive Crown Society membership nurtures growth and connection. Through dynamic programs and the Leading Lady Network Podcast, Krizel inspires women to reign, shine, and claim their power, proving that true beauty and strength begin within. Reign and Shine!

Born to Reign

By Krizel Rodriguez

Wake-Up Call

I remember the hospital room so vividly. It was a brutal reminder of where I was: far from home, far from comfort, stuck in a bizarre reality where the only certainty was uncertainty. When the doctor walked in, his face spoke volumes before he even opened his mouth.

He laid out three prescriptions of antibiotics on a small tray beside my bed. "Krizel, these are the strongest antibiotics in the world. If these don't work, there's nothing more we can do."

At that moment, I felt my heart drop. I'd never before been confronted with the possibility that my body...my life...could be on the line for something as random and rare as this stupid infection. I tried to be brave, but tears built up in my eyes. My mind raced: *How did I get here? Was this really my life? I'm not ready to go! I have so much I want to do, and I have yet to accomplish any of it!*

Not long ago, I was just a woman with big dreams! Someone who was driven and ambitious but also carried a deep, haunting insecurity. It had chipped away at me for years, especially during a marriage that left me feeling trapped, belittled, and voiceless. Daily, I was told I wasn't worthy and that my ideas were stupid. I had always hoped that if I worked harder and became smaller (both physically and emotionally), I might finally be worthy. Maybe I would finally be "seen."

And yet, here I was, on the brink of losing it all. How ironic that the pursuit of being visible had led me to the edge of an invisible diagnosis, a disease so rare that only a few people in the world had it that year. While I sat in that hospital room, I realized I was done. I am done with chasing external validation, done with believing the cruel words of people who had no right to define my worth and done with shrinking myself to fit into someone else's narrative of who I should be.

That evening, I made a promise to myself:

If I make it out of this, I will accomplish all my goals! I will do great things and I will open a business that changes lives.

Years of Feeling Small

To understand why that moment in the hospital mattered so deeply, we have to go back several years when I was married to a man who told me that my ideas were stupid, that I had no value, and that my aspirations were ridiculous. He'd snicker if I dared to mention a goal, as though I'd just proposed a trip to Mars. Over time, I internalized these jabs. They became the background noise of my mind, a constant hum that insisted I wasn't good enough and never would be.

When you hear something enough times, you start to believe it. I began to shrink in every possible way. I silenced my own needs for fear of being ridiculed. I let others make my choices, define my worth, and dictate how my body should look and feel. If I just kept quiet, maybe I'd be lovable. If I just lost weight, perhaps he'd see me in a different light. If I just became less me, I'd possibly become more worthy.

That mindset led me to a consultation for weight-loss surgery. I was convinced that if I changed my appearance, I could finally "earn" the love I wanted. The mistake wasn't in wanting to be healthy but in believing I had to be someone entirely different to deserve visibility, respect, and love.

The Surgery and the Slow-Burn Nightmare

The surgery itself was initially straightforward. I woke up groggy but hopeful. The doctors told me everything had gone well and that I should expect the usual postoperative discomfort. My mind spun: Maybe this was it. Maybe a new day had finally dawned for me—maybe I would become a smaller, more accepted version of myself, and life would magically fall into place.

But something felt off in the weeks that followed. Then, my wounds opened, and more wounds appeared. I went from doctor to doctor, collecting opinions like they were trading cards. Over time, I started questioning my own sanity, wondering if I was somehow overreacting. You try so hard to trust the experts—people who have gone to school for years, who hold your life in their hands—and yet your body is screaming for help, telling you that something is fundamentally wrong.

Two Years of Uncertainty

Two entire years passed like this—twenty-four months of being stuck in medical limbo. Family members told me to get second and third opinions, which I did. But the answers never came.

It's hard to explain what that does to you mentally. You learn to operate in survival mode, to push through days while your mind churns with anxious thoughts at night. Meanwhile, I was still dealing with the emotional toll of a marriage that made me question my value at every turn. When you don't even believe you deserve help, it's easy to let people brush you off.

But eventually, desperation wins out. That's what led me to the Mayo Clinic. I walked into that building carrying not just the physical burden of this unnamed illness but also the emotional scars of feeling invisible in my marriage and in the medical system. The difference was that this time, I refused to be dismissed.

Diagnosis: Mycobacterium Chelonae

After countless tests—blood work, biopsies, cultures, I can't even remember—I finally had a name for my invisible enemy: Mycobacterium

Chelonae. Fewer than ten people worldwide had been diagnosed with it that year. In other words, I'd "won" some sort of twisted cosmic lottery.

Hearing a diagnosis, even a dire one, can be oddly liberating. No one had believed me for two years, yet here was proof: I wasn't imagining it. This thing was real, and it was dangerous. My next question, of course, was, "How do we treat it?" That's when the team of specialists explained that this bacterium was notoriously resistant to most antibiotics.

If this course of antibiotics didn't work, there was nothing else they could do.

The Vow That Changed My Life

I vowed that if I survived, I would never again live my life in the shadows of someone else's expectations. I would never again shrink to be seen, beg to be heard, or contort myself for acceptance.

I made a promise that if I made it out of that hospital, the next chapter of my life would be about living boldly, joyfully, and helping women like me!

Walking Away and Starting Over

The antibiotics did work, although it was an excruciating process. I spent a year hooked up to IV lines. There were moments of hope, then setbacks, then slow improvements, until finally, I was well enough to be discharged. But the real healing journey was just beginning.

You see, recovering from an illness that nearly takes your life is more than a physical process. Your whole worldview is rearranged. You see everything in sharper contrast. So, one morning, I packed my suitcase and walked out. I didn't have a plan, only that vow I had made in the hospital. I was done living a half-life.

This wasn't a cinematic grand exit; it was gritty and terrifying. I questioned myself repeatedly: *Was I making a huge mistake? Could I survive on my own financially? Would I be alone forever? Can I actually run a successful business?* But every time doubt reared its head, I remembered that vow!

Reclaiming My Dreams

After leaving, one of the first things I did was revisit the list of dreams I'd shelved. It was like cracking open a time capsule of who I'd been before life.

They felt like messages from a version of me I had abandoned.

Speak on a stage. Go back to school. Be a mother. Compete in a pageant. Start a business.

Every one of them had once been mocked, dismissed, or forgotten. But now, they were a map back to myself.

So, I started checking them off, one by one.

In 2023, I became a TEDx Speaker. Check!

I enrolled in school. I studied at night after work, after bedtime stories, and I graduated summa cum laude while juggling a full-time job, motherhood, and running a business. Check!

And the pageant? I remembered how I once told my ex I wanted to compete. He said, "Women like you don't wear crowns."

So, I entered. And in 2024, I was crowned Mrs. Texas Plus America. I didn't wear that crown because I fit someone's mold. I wore it because I shattered it. Check!

Business? Oh, just wait!

Becoming a Mother: A New Kind of Love

Amidst all this reinvention, love found me. Real love, the kind that sees you—not the curated version of you, but your flaws, your quirks, your whole story—and chooses you anyway. I call him "Handsome."

Then came another life curveball: the possibility that if I wanted children, I needed to start trying immediately. I was just stepping into my new life, just learning to stand on my own two feet, yet my biological clock was ticking. What about my business? Oh, just wait!

Needles, endless doctor appointments, emotional highs and lows—I went through all of it.

When I finally became pregnant, it felt like a dream. Then, she arrived.

My daughter.
My miracle.
My why.

Bold Business Moves – The Birth Leading Lady Network

As I began owning my voice and taking up space, I came across a statistic that stopped me cold: Women of color make up only 6% of C-suite positions in corporate America. Six percent. That number hit differently now that I had a daughter of my own. How could someone like her—brilliant, bold, beautiful—only have a slim chance at real leadership?

That's when I made a new vow. I wasn't just going to rebuild my life for me—I was going to build something for *her* and for every woman who's ever been overlooked because of her shade, shape, or size.

That's how the **Leading Lady Network** was born. What started as a simple idea—a community for women to be seen and supported—quickly became a movement to rewrite the rules. From it grew **The Leading Lady Network Podcast** and **The Crown Society**, a space where women lead boldly, lift each other higher, and prove that we don't have to fit the mold to wear the crown. We just have to be brave enough to put it on.

Business... CHECK!!

Leading with Your Story

Over the years, I've learned that the heart of leadership and business is rooted in authenticity. Titles, credentials, and accolades may open doors, but actual influence arises when you share your real story—unfiltered, unpolished, and undeniably you. For so long, I hid my struggles, convinced that they made me "less than." Yet, the moment I began telling my story, I discovered the power of vulnerability. People connect to realness, not perfection.

That's why I encourage every woman I coach to dig deep into her experiences. Your challenges, your heartbreaks, your tears—they're not liabilities. They're credentials!! They equip you to lead with compassion, understanding, and courage. They help you see humanity in others and create spaces where people feel safe to show up as they are.

My Core Leadership and Business Lessons

Your story is your platform.

The more I hid from my truth, the smaller I felt. The second I owned my story—scars, struggles, and all—I found my voice. And with that voice came an unexpected opportunity. Don't be afraid to be raw about your journey; there is someone out there waiting to hear it who needs to know they're not alone.

Don't wait for permission.

For too long, I believed I needed someone else to validate my worth. Then I realized the only person who can genuinely crown you is you.

Choose yourself. Appoint yourself. Stop waiting for a nod from someone who doesn't understand your path.

See yourself before expecting others to see you.

True visibility isn't about how many followers you have or who applauds you. It's about looking in the mirror and finally accepting, loving, and respecting the person staring back. Once you do that, it won't matter who chooses to overlook you—you'll know you are worthy of every space you enter.

Your past is a powerful teacher, not a life sentence.

My marriage, my illness, my moments of humiliation—they don't define me. They shaped me, taught me, and fueled my passion to create the Leading Lady Network. Don't bury your past; let it guide you toward a radically different future.

Choose community over competition.

In a world that pits women against each other, I realized there's unimaginable power in collaboration. When you step into a community that champions every shade, shape, and size, you gain a support system that helps you shine brighter than you ever could alone.

A Final Note from My Heart to Yours

Queen, let me remind you: You were never meant to remain invisible or voiceless. If there's one thing my journey has taught me, it's that adversity can become our greatest catalyst for transformation. Maybe you haven't battled a rare disease, or perhaps you have. Maybe your struggle is with self-esteem, finances, heartbreak, or something you can't even name yet. Whatever it is, it's not here to destroy you but to build you.

I hope that my story ignites something in you—a spark, a drive, an unwavering belief that you, too, can rise above every challenge. You, too, can make bold business moves! The Leading Lady Network didn't start with a grand business plan. It began with a promise I made to myself in a hospital room, vowing never to let anyone—myself included—play small in the face of greatness again.

If you take nothing else away from this chapter, let it be this: You have the right to take up space, to speak your truth, to wear your crown proudly. You have the right—and, I dare say, the responsibility—to be visible in every shade, shape, and size you are. The world needs the full, unedited version of you.

And make no mistake—this is just the beginning. For you, for me, for every woman who's ever doubted she could. Together, we can reshape how the world perceives leadership and women in business. Because each of us has a crown, some just need to remember to pick it up and place it on our heads each morning.

One Last Thought

To the woman reading these words, juggling responsibilities and secret dreams, convinced that maybe she's "too old," "too broken," or "too late"—this is your reminder: You're right on time. Your story isn't over; in fact, a vibrant chapter is about to begin. The road ahead may not be easy, but it will be worth it.

So, queen, will you make the same promise I made in that hospital room? Will you vow to never again shrink for the comfort of others? Will you honor every shade, shape, and size of your being and claim your rightful place in this world? I hope you do. Because the moment you crown yourself is the moment the real magic begins.

You are seen. You are heard. You are worthy of reigning in your own life. Now go—shine, lead, and change the world in the way only you can.

Because the world needs you and your business. And I, Krizel, am cheering for you every step of the way.

JOIN THE MOVEMENT!
#BAUW

Becoming An Unstoppable Woman
With She Rises Studios

She Rises Studios was founded by Hanna Olivas and Adriana Luna Carlos, the mother-daughter duo, in mid-2020 as they saw a need to help empower women worldwide. They are the podcast hosts of the *She Rises Studios Podcast* and Amazon best-selling authors and motivational speakers who travel the world. Hanna and Adriana are the movement creators of #BAUW - Becoming An Unstoppable Woman: The movement has been created to universally impact women of all ages, at whatever stage of life, to overcome insecurities, and adversities, and develop an unstoppable mindset. She Rises Studios educates, celebrates, and empowers women globally.

We Are
SHE RISES STUDIOS
A real-life community of women working to become the best version of themselves to change their lives and make the world a better place.

LEARN MORE

Looking to Join Us in our Next Anthology or Publish YOUR Own?

She Rises Studios Publishing offers full-service publishing, marketing, book tour, and campaign services. For more information, contact info@sherisesstudios.com

We are always looking for women who want to share their stories and expertise and feature their businesses on our podcasts, in our books, and in our magazines.

SEE WHAT WE DO

OUR PODCAST

OUR BOOKS

OUR SERVICES

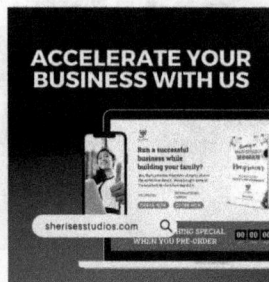

Be featured in the Becoming An Unstoppable Woman magazine, published in 13 countries and sold in all major retailers. Get the visibility you need to LEVEL UP in your business!

Have your own TV show streamed across major platforms like Roku TV, Amazon Fire Stick, Apple TV and more!

Learn to leverage your expertise. Build your online presence and grow your audience with FENIX TV.
https://fenixtv.sherisesstudios.com/

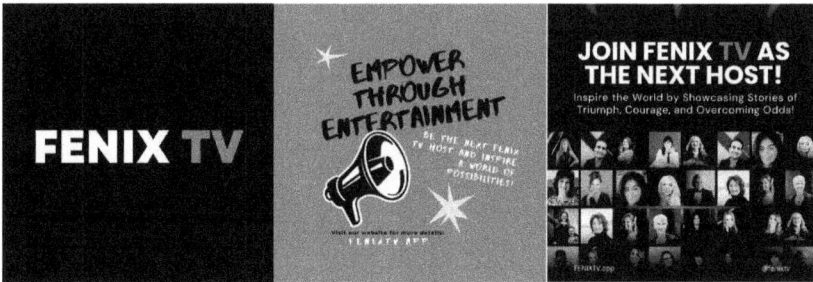

Visit www.SheRisesStudios.com to see how YOU can join the #BAUW movement and help your community to achieve the UNSTOPPABLE mindset.

Have you checked out the *She Rises Studios Podcast?*

Find us on all MAJOR platforms: Spotify, IHeartRadio, Apple Podcasts, Google Podcasts, etc.

Looking to become a sponsor or build a partnership?

Email us at info@sherisesstudios.com

SHE RISES
S T U D I O S

www.ingramcontent.com/pod-product-compliance
Lightning Source LLC
Chambersburg PA
CBHW071704210326
41597CB00017B/2332